Preface

A Step Ahead: ICSE Social Studies is a series of Social Studies books for classes 3 to 5. This series is based on the latest curriculum and syllabus of the Council for the Indian School Certificate Examinations (CISCE).

The series introduces the learners to their past through their heritage, family system, changes around them, national and cultural events on the basis of evidences and varied sources to help them to make a connection with the present.

This series has been designed to present the concepts in a simple yet engaging manner. Each chapter has exercises and activities that would make learning more meaningful and enable the learners to make connections with the wider world.

Features of the series:

- Warm Up: Lead-in to the chapter by taking the children from the known and familiar to the unknown and unfamiliar
- Let's Do: In-text activities to assess the grasp of the concept
- Let's Talk: In-text discussions for the class
- Did You Know?: Snippets of information based on the concept but beyond the text
- Points to be Noted: Recapitulation of the important points covered
- Words to Know: Meaning of new and unfamiliar words
- Think and Discuss: Covers application based questions that motivate students to think critically beyond the syllabus
- Life Skills: Links various skills as enunciated in the syllabus
- Creative Work: Activities to facilitate the learners to express the concepts learnt
- Project Work: Integrates activities to reinforce the topic learnt
- 360° Holistic Progress Card: Provided for every chapter at the end of the book

Additional features:

- 21st Century Skills comprising Learning Skills, Literary Skills and Life Skills as envisioned in the NEP 2020 are duly incorporated
- Sustainable Development Goals (SDGs) are addressed by way of embedded tasks, projects and activities in the chapters

The series has been developed with great care for effective teaching and leaning of Social Studies in the classroom and beyond.

Suggestions for the improvement of the series will be gratefully acknowledged.

Syllabus

Concepts	Learning Outcomes
Theme 1: Evolution of Mankind 1. Evolution of Mankind • Brief introduction of story of human evolution on Earth • Sources/Evidences (fossils, bones, utensils, cave paintings, tools, etc.) 2. The Four Stone Ages • Paleolithic • Mesolithic • Neolithic • Chalcolithic 3. The Iron Age 4. Evolution of Transport and Communication • Invention of the wheel and beginning of transport • Reaching distant places • Trade and voyages • Modern means of transport • Need for writing. • Use of pigeons • Invention of telephone and telegraph • Printing press, • Computers • Satellites	• Identify the stages of the evolution of mankind • List the sources of evidence of man's evolution • Identify, compare and contrast the features of the four stone ages • Identify and reflect on the stages of evolution in modes and system of transport and communication • Discuss and appreciate the developmental process of human life on Earth
Theme 2: The Constitution of India–Basic Features 1. The Indian Constitution (formation, nature, need, and guiding principles).\ 2. Fundamental Rights and Duties 3. Features of the democratic form of government 4. Importance of Elections 5. Responsibilities of a citizen in a democratic polity	• Analyse the need and importance of a Constitution • Identify and list the fundamental rights and duties as a good citizen • State the features of the Indian government • Illustrate the stages of election • Discuss the importance of choosing the right representative • Describe the responsibilities of a citizen in a democratic polity
Theme 3: The Earth--Its Geographical Features 1. Locating Places on the Earth • Latitudes (introduction, characteristics, important latitudes) • Longitudes (introduction, characteristics) 2. Weather and Climate • Difference between weather and climate • Factors that affect climate of a place 3. Solar and Lunar Eclipse 4. Major Temperature Zones of the Earth • Torrid • Temperature • Frigid	• Discuss the terms– latitude and longitude • Identify different places on the map with the help of latitude and longitude • Explain the concept of the major temperature zones • Differentiate between weather and climate • Enlist the major temperature zones • Identify climates and find out the reasons for climatic changes

Theme 4: India - A Diverse Country 1. India: Location and Extent 2. India and its Neighbouring Countries 3. Climate of India (Different Seasons) • Summer season • Continents and oceans • Rainy (Monsoon) season 4. Natural Vegetation • Tropical evergreen • Deciduous (monsoon forest) • Thorn and Scrub • Montane forest	• Identify and locate India on the world map • Locate neighbouring countries of India on the map • Compare the size of India with neighbouring countries • Relate climate to the different regions of the country • Identify various types of vegetation found in India • Relate and compare vegetation and climate in different parts of India • Describe importance of vegetation and its conservation
Theme 5: The Environment– Major Concerns 1. Components of the Environment (biotic and abiotic) 2. Interdependence of and between different regions of the world 3. Impact of local events on global environment, global warming 4. Natural Disasters • Earthquake » Cyclones » Floods » Droughts » Volcanic eruptions » Landslides 5. Effects and Precautions of Natural Disasters	• Identify the components of the environment • Discuss critically the reasons for interdependence of people living in different parts of the world • Explain reasons for ozone depletion • Describe change in temperature due to global warming and its impacts • Demonstrate rules to be followed to reduce pollution • Discuss the precautions that need to be taken at the time of natural disaster
Theme 6: Natural Resources 1. Meaning of Resources 2. Renewable and Non-Renewable resources 3. Renewable Resources – (air, water, soil, plants, animals, solar energy and wind energy) – brief description 4. Non-Renewable Resources – (Coal and Petroleum, Minerals) – brief description	• Discuss and understand the term resources • Compare and differentiate between renewable and non-renewable resources • Identify and enlist the resources • Discuss the use of resources in life • Suggest ways to conserve resources
Theme 7: Major Occupations in India 1. Agriculture • Types of crops, food crop, cash crop • Development of agriculture • Livestock rearing (map work) 2. Industries • Major industries in India • Large-scale industries and small-scale industries • Other industries	• Differentiate between man-made and machine made products • Enlist the large-scale industries in our country • Differentiate between raw material and finished products • Compare old and new methods of farming • Discuss our dependence on industries in day-to-day life • Appreciate the skills of persons involved in crafts

Key

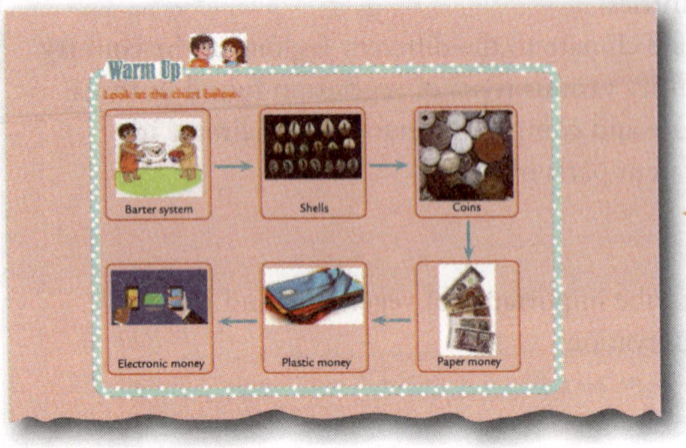

Each chapter starts with **Warm Up**, a lead-in to the chapter

Topics arranged under heads and sub-heads for better understanding

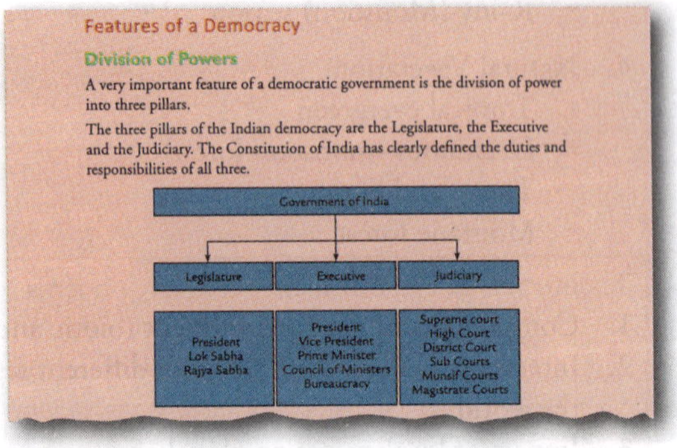

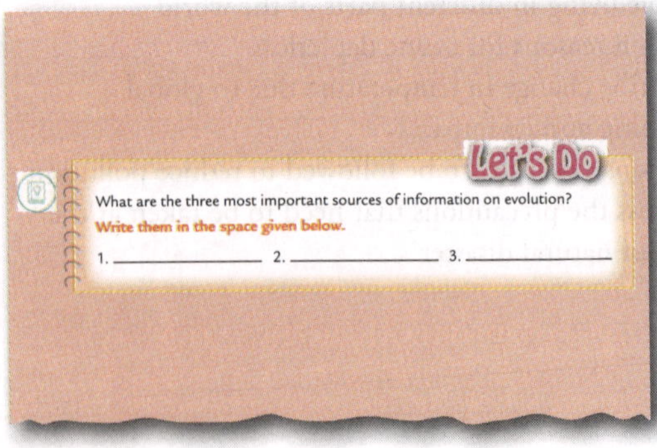

Let's Do are in-text activities to assess the grasp of the concept

Did You Know are snippets of information based on the concept but beyond the syllabus

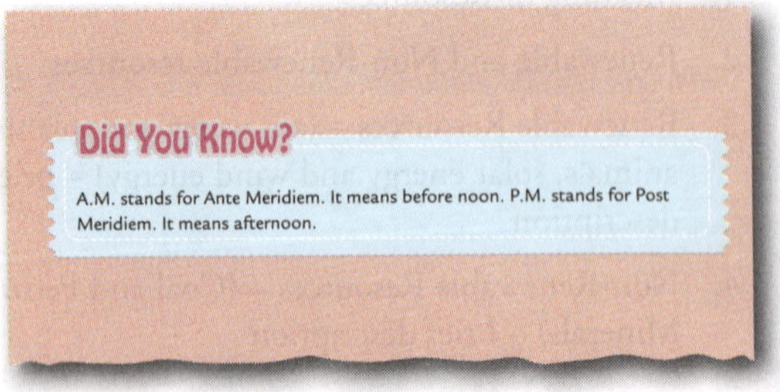

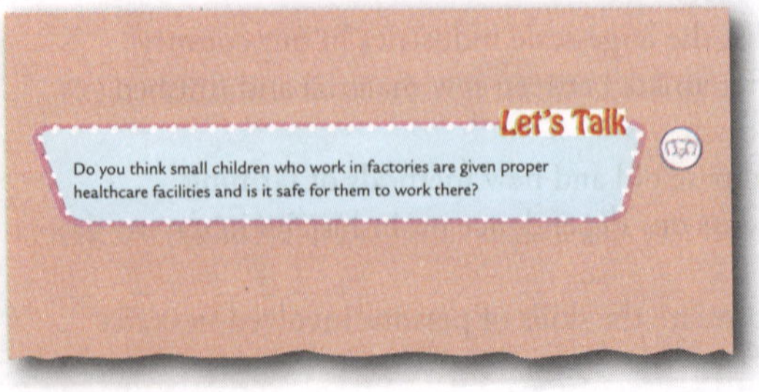

Let's Talk are in-text discussions for the class

Features

Points to be Noted are recapitulation of all the important concepts discussed in the chapter

Points to be Noted

- Early humans started travelling because of various reasons like climate change, for food, hospitable lands for farming, etc.
- The wheel, invented in the Neolithic Age, made it easy to move objects and people.
- Traders and sailors travelled in search of new lands and markets, to spread religion and to gain control over the newly founded lands.
- Modern means of transport are land, water and air transport.
- Early humans could express thoughts and feelings by means of speech or by signs or gestures.
- The earliest form of writing was pictographs - symbols which represented objects.
- Before the advancement of technology, messenger pigeons were used to carry messages or letters to war grounds.
- Various means of communication were invented like telegraphs, telephones, computers and satellites.

Words to Know are meanings of terms used in the chapter

Words to Know

Principle: a rule of conduct based on beliefs of what is right and wrong
Fundamental: the most central and important part of something
Preamble: an introduction to a book or a written document
Procedures: established or official ways of doing something
Policy: a plan of action of a government

All types of questions adequately covered

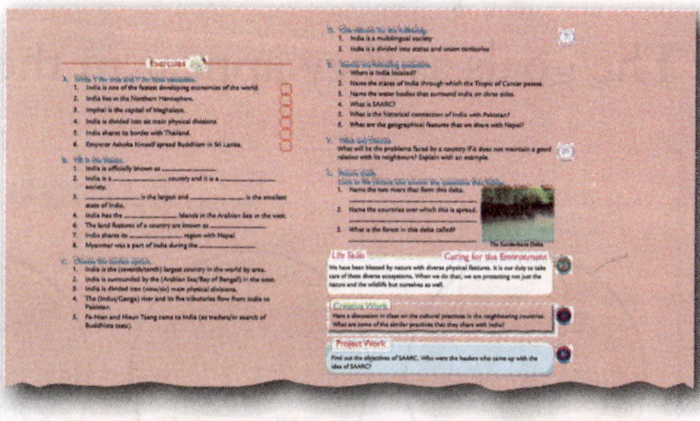

Life Skills as enunciated in the syllabus

Life Skills — Equality

The Preamble says that equal and fair opportunity should be given to everyone irrespective of their caste, religion, race and colour. So, to treat everyone around us with equality and respect is not only a virtue but is something that the law of the country instructs us to do. When we treat everyone with equal respect, the country becomes stronger as the divisions get reduced.

Creative Work are activities to enable learners to apply the concepts learnt creatively

Creative Work

The sign of a healthy democracy is the ability to consider all points of view before any decision is arrived at. That is what you see our parliamentarians doing in the Lok Sabha or the state leaders in the assembly.
Have a class debate on the topic, 'Directive Principles are more important than Fundamental Rights'. One group will be for the motion, the other will be against the motion.

Project Work integrates activities to reinforce the topics learnt in the chapter

Project Work

In India and the US, the President is the head of the State. Find out what their functions are in each country. Also, find out who holds the real power in each of these countries.

The New Education Policy 2020 spells out the need to inculcate in the learners the 21st Century Skills which are a set of skills and abilities aimed at enabling individuals to be relevant and to cope up with the challenges of the new era.

The skills as they appear in the series are indicated by the following icons.

21st Century Skills

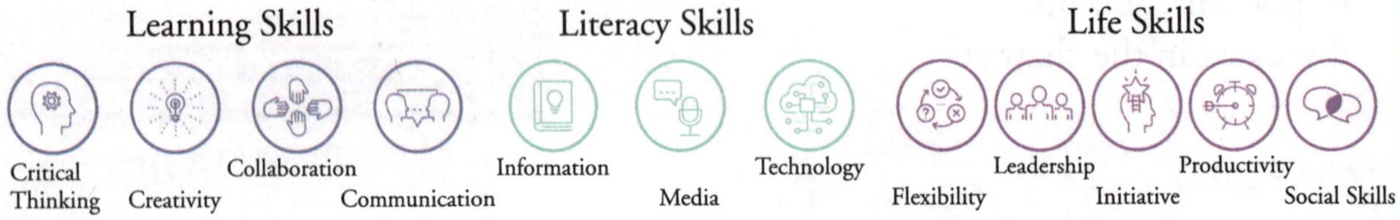

The Sustainable Development Goals (SDGs) as mapped out by NITI Aayog to bring to fruition the Agenda 2030 of the Government of India have also been comprehensively addressed in the series.

The goals as they appear in the series are indicated by the following icons.

Sustainable Development Goals

Contents

Theme 1 : Evolution of Mankind

1 Evolution of Humans

Warm Up

Look at the chart given below.

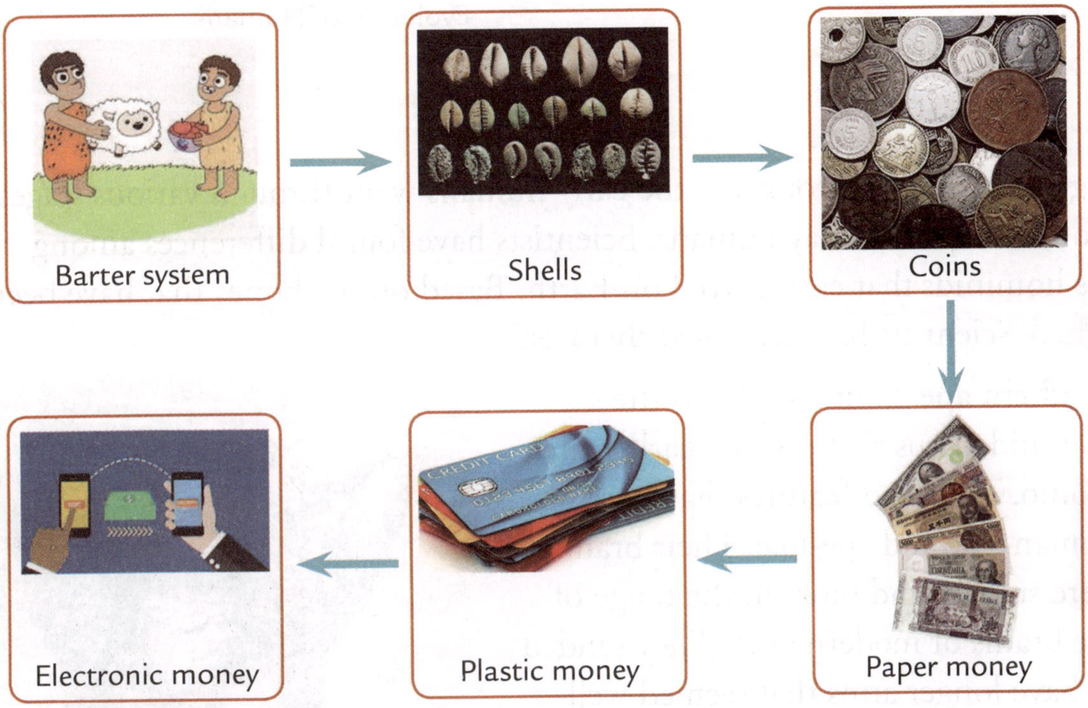

The above activity tells you how money has evolved through history. Similarly, in this chapter we shall study how humans have evolved through time.

The Story of Human Evolution

Different organisms have developed from their earlier forms during the course of time and this process is termed as evolution. Hominids, the earliest of humans are known to have evolved about six to eight million years ago. They are believed to have originated from ape-like creatures who used to walk on all four limbs and lived on trees. Then, around two million years ago, early humans first migrated out of

Africa into Asia long before the modern humans known as Homo sapiens appeared in the same continent. They stood upright and started walking on two limbs. They learned to hunt and started making tools. They used to live in small, nomadic groups. This process of change or evolution in humans is known as human evolution.

Evolution of Humans

The Stages in Human Evolution

During the process of evolution, the early humans went through various stages to become the present-day humans. Scientists have found differences among various hominids that earlier lived on Earth. Based on the bones that have been unearthed, scientists have classified them as:

Reconstruction of a male Southern ape

- **Southern ape**: Southern ape is the hominid genus that evolved earlier than Homo. They had features that were both human-like and ape-like. Their brains were smaller and more in the range of the brains of modern apes. They tended to have longer arms that seemed well-suited to climbing. They walked erect and were bipedal i.e., walked on two feet. Their teeth were larger than human teeth, but smaller than the teeth of apes. The size of males was larger than females. They lived on the ground and used stone weapons for hunting.

Reconstruction of a Homo erectus boy

- **Homo erectus**: They belong to genus Homo, perhaps an ancestor of modern humans. Homo erectus was a human of medium stature that walked upright. The brain was smaller, the forehead was receded, and the nose and jaws were wide. They had teeth larger than in modern humans. Homo erectus appears to have been the first human species to control fire. They used to live in communities, used weapons and tools made of wood, bone and stone. They were believed to have flourished the longest time span, up to two million years.

Reconstruction of a Neanderthal man

- **Homo sapiens Neanderthalensis or the Neanderthal**: Neanderthals co-existed with modern humans for a long period of time before eventually becoming extinct about 28,000 years ago. The word, Neanderthalensis, is based on the location where the first major specimen was discovered in 1856—the Neander Valley in Germany. Their brain size was larger than the average modern human brain. They were shorter in height but their teeth were larger in size than ours. They built hearths and were able to control fire to cook food and for protection. They used to wear animal skins. Caves were often used as shelters but open air shelters were also constructed.

Reconstruction of an early Homo sapien

- **Homo sapiens**: Homo sapiens is the species to which all modern human beings belong. Homo sapiens is one of several species grouped into the genus Homo, but it is the only one that is not extinct. They had a defined skull, rounded at the back, with small teeth, smaller jaws and the size of the brain was big. They used tools like needles and weapons made of copper and iron.

Did You Know?

As humans moved away from Africa and the Equator, we developed variations in skin tone (lighter skin absorbs more vitamin D), hair texture, and facial features.

Sources or Evidences

Early humans made and used various things in the past. We get to know this from the various sources unearthed which include bones, tools and other evidences such as footprints, constructions made of stone and brick, paintings and sculpture left by the early humans. People who study such objects are known as archaeologists. These remains laid buried which preserved them naturally till they were found and studied by archaeologists. These remains help us to learn about the physical appearance of early humans, how they lived at that period of time and the environment that existed at that time.

Fossils

The fossil of a dodo

The primary source of evidence of human evolution are fossils. The trace of fossils and other sources from Africa and Eurasia provide important information about the ancient past. Fossils are the remains of dead plants and animals which were buried inside the Earth a long time ago. The study of fossils is known as palaeontology and people who study fossils are known a palaeontologists. They study the size and shape of the bone and inform us of the changes that took place in the human body during the process of evolution.

Cave Paintings

Cave painting of early humans at Bhimbetka, Madhya Pradesh

Cave paintings are another source or evidence which provide a great detail about the lives of early humans. The most common subjects in cave paintings are activities of everyday lives of early humans like food gathering, hunting and of worshipping. Such paintings can be found in Lascaux in France, Bhimbetka in India, El Castillo in Spain and Magura in Bulgaria. These paintings depict scenes mainly of dancing, playing music, hunting, horse and elephant riding, decorating bodies and honey collecting. Animals like tigers, lions, wild boar, elephants, dogs and crocodiles have also been portrayed in the paintings. The colours in these paintings are obtained from rocks and minerals which were locally available at that time.

Tools and Utensils

In the earlier times, humans made simple hand-axes carved out of stones. They attached wood to bones of animals to be used as tools. They also sharpened sticks to use as hunting spears, arrowheads and knives. They used stone tools to cut, pound, and crush things. It also helped them in extracting meat from animals.

Tools used by early humans

Various vessels made from stones, clay and bronze have been found at the excavation sites. Two such sites are Harappa and Mohenjo-Daro.

Let's Do

What are the three most important sources of information on evolution?

Write them in the space given below.

1. ______________ 2. ______________ 3. ______________

How Did Early Humans Communicate?

Early humans used to communicate through gestures and signs. Fire and smoke were used by them to give signals. As the vocal tract in humans developed, they began to develop languages using different sounds. The cave paintings and pictographs on wet clay, were one way of communicating. They used to draw their actions or feelings and then used this to communicate with each other.

Let's Talk

What do you think the early humans were trying to communicate through their paintings?

Hunting and Food Gathering

Before humans started to rear cattle and began farming, they were dependent on the animal and plant resources around them for food. They hunted animals for the meat. After fire was discovered, the meat was cooked over it. They also collected fruits, roots, nuts and seeds from plants. That is why they were called as hunter-gatherers.

A painting of hunter-gatherers

The Trading System

The trade system was in existence way before humans began to use coins. Early humans learned to make of weapons and tools, grow crops and rear cattle. When they found a need to exchange goods, a system was introduced in which goods and services were exchanged for other goods and services. This system came to known as barter system. The history of bartering dates all the way back to 6000 BC. Long-distance trade in those early times was made possible only after the invention of the wheel about which you will read in the further chapters.

Points to be Noted

- Hominids, the earliest of humans, used to walk on all four limbs and lived on trees.
- The process of evolution from ape-like creatures to humans is known as human evolution.
- There are various stages of human evolution. Some of them are: Southern ape, Homo erectus, Homo sapiens Neanderthalensis or the Neanderthal and Homo sapiens.
- Archaeologists study the evidences unearthed to trace human evolution.
- The primary source of evidence of human evolution are fossils.
- The most common subjects in cave paintings were activities of everyday lives of early humans like food gathering, hunting and worshipping.
- Stone tools were used to cut, pound and crush things.
- Early humans used to communicate through gestures and signs. Fire was used to give signals.
- They used to hunt animals and gather food from plants before they discovered farming.
- Barter system was used to trade goods and services to get other goods and services in return.

Words to Know

Originated: started

Migrated: travelled from one part of the world to another

Unearthed: find (something) in the ground by digging

Erect: standing straight

Extinct: died out or no longer alive

Evidence: proof

Extracting: taking something out, especially with difficulty

Excavation sites: the areas which are dug out for study

Pictographs: representation of data or information using images

Exercises

A. Write T for true and F for false sentences.

1. Southern apes are the species to which all modern human beings belong. ☐
2. Fossils are the remains of dead plants and animals. ☐
3. Early humans used to communicate through writing. ☐
4. Coins were used by early humans from the beginning for trading. ☐
5. Barter system is about the exchange of human beings. ☐

B. Fill in the blanks.

1. The modern humans are known as __________.
2. This process of change or evolution in humans is known as __________.
3. __________ used to live in communities, used weapons and tools made of wood, bone and stone.
4. People who study fossils are known as __________.
5. Cave paintings in India can be found in __________.
6. In the __________ goods and services were exchanged for other goods and services.

C. Choose the correct word.

1. The earlier humans evolved (six to eight/three to four) million years ago.
2. Homo sapiens had (larger/smaller) teeth.
3. (Fossils/Modern humans) give us information about the ancient past.

4. The colours for ancient rock paintings were obtained from (rocks and minerals/stems of plants).
5. As the (brain size/vocal tract) developed, humans began to develop languages using different sounds.
6. Humans used to eat (raw meat and plants/only plants) before fire was discovered.

D. Answer in one word.

1. The process by which organisms developed from their earlier form: ____________
2. The hominid genus that evolved earlier than Homo: ____________
3. People who study evidences from the past: ____________
4. The study of fossils: ____________
5. Humans who hunted animals and gathered fruits from plants: ____________

E. Answer the following questions.

1. What is evolution?
2. What are the various stages of human evolution?
3. Write in detail about the sources which trace human evolution.
4. What are fossils? Who are the people who study about fossils?
5. How did early humans communicate with each other?
6. What is barter system? Why was it used?

F. Think and Discuss

1. How different would it have been if humans had not evolved?
2. Do you think modern humans can be called as hunter-gatherers? Why or why not?

G. Picture Study

Look at the pictures and answer the questions that follow.

1. What do you see in the pictures?

2. Why were they made by early humans?

3. From where do you think they got the colours?

Life Skills — Communication

Early humans also understood the need of communicating. That is why they left messages on their paintings. This teaches us the importance of communication in a society. It is only when we communicate that we can understand each other. That is how we grow as a society.

Creative Work

Find out more about the cave paintings found across the world. Find out their similarities and write your observations in the notebook.

Project Work

Find out more about the evidences which anthropologists have unearthed. Also collect their pictures and mention where they were found.

2 The Stone Age and the Iron Age

Warm Up

Look at the image and answer the questions.

- What is this?
  ____
- Who lives inside it?
  ____
- Do you think early humans used to live inside them?
  Yes ☐ No ☐

The Stone Age

Yes, evidence suggests that early humans lived in caves. During this time, the tools, weapons and utensils used by them were simple and made of stones. Hence, the age in which stone tools were used by early humans is termed as Stone Age. The Stone Age lasted for 2.5 million years and ended when humans began to work with metals and started making tools and weapons from bronze.

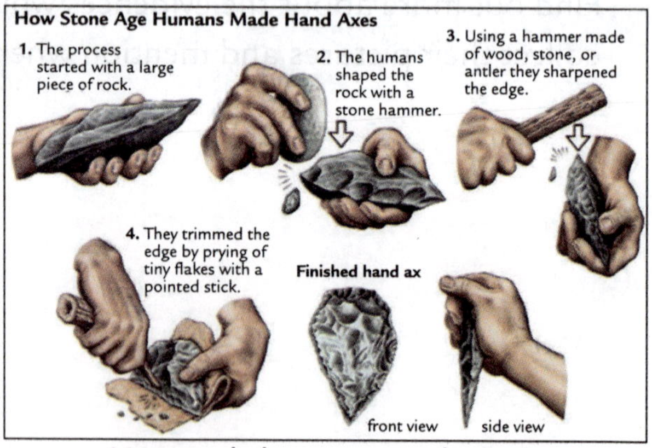

How early humans made tools

The Stone Age is further divided into four ages: Palaeolithic, Mesolithic, Neolithic and Chalcolithic.

The Palaeolithic Age

The word palaeolithic is made up of two words, 'palaeos' means old and 'lithos' means stone. Hence, this age is also known as the Old Stone Age. This age was the earliest period of human development, which lasted until 8000 BC. During the Palaeolithic period humans were hunters and food-gatherers. They had not started farming so they used to survive on roots of trees and fruits. They lived in caves, near rivers and in animal skin tents, to protect themselves from different weather conditions and animals. They used simple stone tools for hunting and other purposes. These tools were made from large and small scrapers, hammer stones, choppers, awls, etc. Tools used in Palaeolithic era were mainly cleavers, choppers, and hand axes. These tools were mainly used for cutting, digging and skinning the prey. Tools of this age was majorly dependent on flakes which were used to make bores, points and scrapers.

An artist's impression of early humans living in caves

Stones used in Palaeolithic Age for axe

The Palaeolithic people primarily used hand-axes as weapons which were used for hunting as well as for protection. This was their main or core tool, which was made by chipping the stone to form a cutting edge. The early Stone Age humans were nomads as they moved from place to place in search of food. They lived in groups of 20-30 people. Outsiders were looked upon as enemies. One male member was considered as the leader in every group. They had no knowledge of house building and agriculture. Hence, communities or societies were not developed in this period.

The Mesolithic Age

Mesolithic Age, also called Middle Stone Age, existed between the Paleolithic Age (Old Stone Age) and the Neolithic Age (New Stone Age), with its polished stone tools. When the climate began to become warm, humans started settling at one place giving rise to societies and communities. People started building small wooden settlements. Heavy stone tools were

Mesolithic blades

replaced by smaller and lighter tools known as microliths which were triangular in shape and were attached to sticks made of wood and bones to make arrows or spears. Many microliths made of chert, jasper, quartzite and flint have been found that belong to this age. Humans began to domesticate animals like dogs, goats and sheep for different purposes. The people of this age practised painting. Their paintings depicted birds, animals and human beings. Towards the end of the Mesolithic Age early humans learnt about agriculture.

Let's Talk

If you are asked to live like early humans, would it be easy for you to live such a lifestyle?

The Neolithic Age

The Neolithic Age or the New Stone Age, was the third Stone Age. In India, it spanned from around 7,000 BC to 1,000 BC. In the Neolithic Age, humans turned from food gatherers to food producers. It also witnessed the use of pottery for the first time. The people used microlithic blades in addition to tools made of polished stones. They used stone hoes and digging sticks for digging the ground. They also used tools and weapons made of bones.

An artist's impression of life in Neolithic Age

The people primarily used axes as weapons. The North-western part of Neolithic settlement in India used rectangular axes having curved cutting edge. The Southern part used axes with oval sides and pointed butt while polished stone axes with rectangular butt and shouldered hoes were used in the North-eastern part.

Tool used for cultivation in the Neolithic Age

The wheel was a remarkable invention of this period. It helped in pottery making and replaced handmade pots. These pots were now baked in furnaces, glazed and decorated. The wheel also helped in spinning and weaving. Cotton and wool were used to make clothes and shells and bone were being used for ornaments.

The people of the Neolithic Age lived in rectangular or circular houses which were made of mud and reed. They cultivated ragi, horse gram, cotton, rice, wheat and barley and hence, were termed as food producers.

The Chalcolithic Age

The Chalcolithic Age is the age that existed between the Neolithic Age and the Bronze Age. In this age, humans began to use copper tools as well as stone tools till about 2000 BC. Copper metallurgy began in northern Mesopotamia. Copper tools were much stronger and more durable than the stone tools. Crops grown by Chalcolithic farmers included barley, wheat and pulses. People began trade in animals, copper and silver ores, basalt bowls, timber, and resins. Houses built by Chalcolithic farmers were constructed of stone or mud brick. This age also marks the beginning of some form of administrative organisations among the communities.

House made of wood and mud brick

The Bronze Age

The Bronze Age marks the beginning of the use of bronze for making tools and weapons. Humans learned to make bronze by mixing copper and tin. The

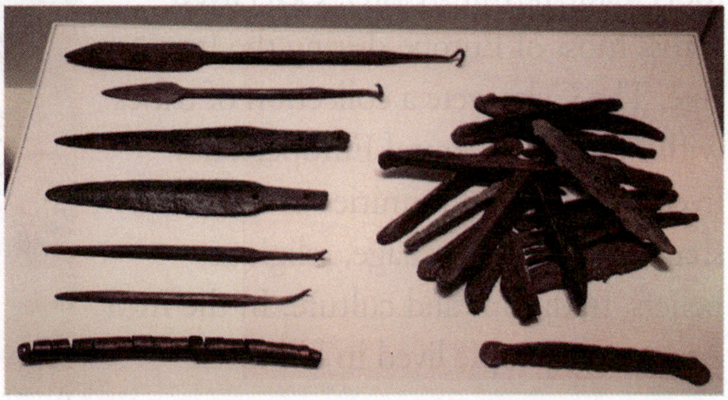

Tools of the Bronze Age

tools and weapons were made of bronze as they were stronger than stone. Utensils were also made of bronze. Many new inventions continued to take place in this age. This age was followed by the Iron Age, the age in which people began to use iron to make tools and weapons.

Did You Know?

Bronze is made by heating the metals tin and iron and mixing them together.

The Iron Age

An artist's impression of people making iron tools

The Iron Age began around 1200 BC in the Mediterranean region and Near East and ended in 550 BC. It marks the beginning of the period in the history of humankind when iron came to be used for making tools, weapons, utensils and other artefacts. In this age, people across much of Europe, Asia and parts of Africa began making tools and weapons from iron and steel.

The earlier iron tools seemed less durable than copper and bronze tools. The use of iron became more widespread after people learned to make steel, a much sturdier metal, by heating iron with carbon. They learned that steel weapons were sharper and stronger than the earlier bronze or stone weapons.

Lifestyle of Humans during the Iron Age

An artist's impression of houses in the Iron Age

Life in the Iron Age in Europe was primarily rural and agricultural. Iron tools made farming easier. Celts lived across most of Europe during the Iron Age. The Celts were a collection of tribes with origins in Central Europe. They lived in small communities or clans and shared a similar language, religious beliefs, traditions and culture. In the Iron Age, many people lived in hill forts.

The forts were surrounded by walls and ditches and warriors defended their people from enemy attacks. Inside the hill forts, families lived in round houses. These were simple one-roomed homes with a pointed thatched roof and walls made a mixture of mud and twigs.

An artist's impression of farming in the Iron Age

Iron Age farmers grew crops and vegetables. They kept geese, goats and pigs and had large herds of cows and flocks of sheep.

Why Did Early Humans Use Iron?

- Iron was stronger than bronze and copper. So the tools made with it were stronger.
- Tin, which was used to make bronze, was not widely available, so people started searching for alternatives.
- Iron did not need any other metal to be mixed with it. It was just heated till it became soft to be hammered into different shapes.
- It was widely available in most parts of the world.

How Has Iron Changed the World?

- Iron was used to make strong tools for farming. Iron ploughs were used to dig deeper into the grounds.
- Better farming techniques increased production, which made it possible to sell and exchange surplus crops. People also started making axes to cut wood and sickles to harvest crops.

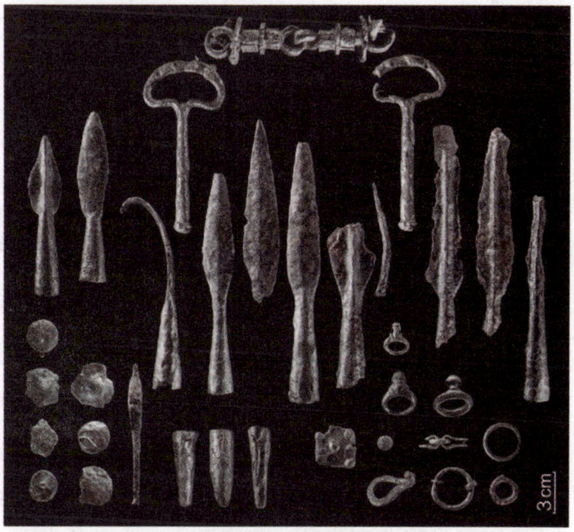

Arms used in the Iron Age

- Iron was used to make swords, nails, spears, arrowheads and pots. These weapons were stronger and were used by armies to fight battles.
- With the increase in food productivity and trade, there came about division of labour. People started doing other things which gave rise to urban cities and civilizations came into existence. The two civilizations which existed before the Iron Age were the Greek and Roman Civilizations. These civilizations were highly developed in trade, art, writing and architecture. Later, iron also helped in the rise of the Industrial Revolution.
- Iron also helped in replacing the barter system of exchanging goods and services into buying goods and services with money. Coins were introduced. Earlier, coins were made of iron and bronze but later they came to be made from silver and gold.

Early coins made of iron and silver

Let's Do

Name some things that are made of iron around you.

1. ____________ 2. ____________ 3. ____________ 4. ____________

Points to be Noted

- The age in which stone tools were used by early humans is termed as Stone Age.
- In the Old Stone Age, humans lived in caves. They were known as hunter-gatherers.
- Flaked tools were used to make bores, points and scrapers.
- In the Mesolithic Age, humans used polished stone tools and they started building small wooden settlements.

- The Neolithic Age saw humans turning into food producer from food gatherer. The wheel was the most remarkable invention of this age.
- Houses built by Chalcolithic farmers were in chain building pattern and constructed of stone or mud brick. Chalcolithic farmers grew barley, wheat, and pulses.
- The Iron Age is that period when human beings began to use iron for making tools, weapons, utensils and many other useful things.

Words to Know

Nomads: people that move from place to place without settling in any area

Hoe: a garden tool with a long handle that is used for turning the soil and for removing plants that you do not want

Domesticate: to train an animal to live with or work for humans

Reed: a tall plant, like grass, that grows in or near water

Metallurgy: the study of metals and their uses

Domesticate: to train an animal to live with or work for humans

Exercises

A. Write T for true and F for false statements.

1. The Stone Age is divided into six ages. ☐
2. The Palaeolithic Age was the earliest period of human development. ☐
3. Heavy stone tools were replaced by smaller and lighter tools known as microliths. ☐
4. Towards the end of the Neolithic Age, humans learnt farming. ☐
5. The people of the Neolithic Age lived in rectangular or circular houses. ☐
6. The use of iron helped in the Industrial Revolution. ☐

B. Fill in the blanks.

1. The Palaeolithic people primarily used hand-axes as weapons which were used for __________ as well as for __________.
2. One __________ member was considered as the leader in every group.

3. Humans began to domesticate animals in the ________.
4. The Neolithic Age saw humans turning into ________ from ________.
5. In the Neolithic Age, pots were baked in ________, glazed and ________.
6. The Iron Age began around ________ BC in the ________ region.

C. Choose the correct answer.

1. The Old Stone Age is known as (Chalcolithic Age/Palaeolithic Age).
2. In the Mesolithic Age people began (fishing/pottery).
3. In the Neolithic Age humans became (scientists/food producers).
4. Pottery was first introduced in the (Mesolithic Age/Neolithic Age).
5. The (wheel/arrow) was first invented in the Neolithic period.

D. Answer the following in one or two words.

1. The main tool of the Palaeolithic people: ________
2. The age when humans began to domesticate animals: ________
3. The age when humans became food producers: ________
4. The age when humans began to use copper: ________
5. The age when coins were introduced: ________

E. Answer the following questions.

1. What is the Stone Age? How many Stone Ages are there?
2. What do you understand by the term Palaeolithic Age? How did people live in this age?
3. What were microliths? How were they better than the earlier tools?
4. How did the discovery of wheel change the life of early humans?
5. Write a short note on the Iron Age.

F. Think and Discuss

1. Why do you think the Neolithic Age was an important age?
2. What would the world be like without wheels?

G. Picture Study

Look at the picture and answer the following questions.

1. What is this? ____________________
2. During which dynasty was it built? ____________________
3. Who was the founder of this empire? ____________________

   (This Empire was a geographically extensive Iron Age historical power in ancient India, from 322–185 BC. Have a discussion about it in class.)

Life Skills — Leadership

Leadership is important for a society to grow. The leaders inspire the members and help them in working together in uplifting the community or society. A good leader tries to bring out the best from each member and ensures that all actions lead to the development of the society.

Creative Work

Form small groups and organise a skit to show how people lived in the Stone Age and Iron Age.

Project Work

On a chart paper draw a timeline of developments which took place from the Stone Age to Iron Age.

3 Evolution of Transport and Communication

Warm Up

Tick (✓) the things that run on wheels.

 ☐	 ☐	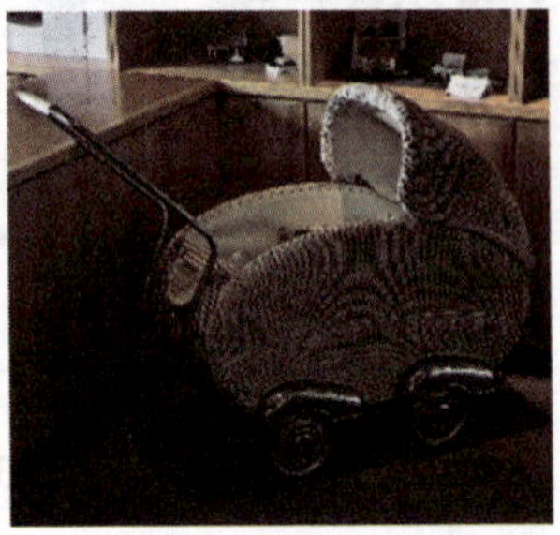 ☐
 ☐	 ☐	 ☐

All these run on wheels.

Evolution of Transport

People in the Neolithic Age started to travel and wander around in search of better locations for food and hospitable lands for farming, etc.

Earlier, humans used to drag or slide heavy objects to move them from one place to another. They must have realised that rolling things were easier and made them move faster. They might have used rollers made of wood to carry heavy objects.

The Invention of Wheel

The beginning of transportation began with the invention of the wheel. The oldest wheel was discovered in Mesopotamia and is believed to be over 5,500 years old. It was not used for transportation, though, but rather as a potter's wheel. Initially, wheels were made of stone and wood and were used on carts and chariots pulled by oxen or horses. But humans discovered that a wheel powered by people, animals, wind or flowing water can be put to many other uses. Muscle power of horses and bullocks was used to pull carts. Boats used the muscle power to move oars. Sail boats used the power of wind to move.

A depiction of cart with wheels in olden times

The invention of wheel made travelling easier and quicker. Later, wheels were also used for spinning and weaving clothes.

Let's Talk

Would travelling have been convenient if wheels were not invented?

Trade and Voyage

The invention and widespread adoption of the wagon had an immediate and dramatic effect on societies throughout the Middle East and Europe. It drastically increased the production of crops. It became easy for farmers to move the heavy loads of fertilizer, seeds and crops. People could now easily settle down in different places using carts and wagons. The production was taken to the markets for trade. Though the invention of the wheel made it possible for humans to travel from one place to another, it was time consuming and was only better to cover short distances. Later, the invention of ships helped in expanding trades to distant places through the sea route.

After the invention of the wheel, traders and sailors travelled in search of new lands and markets, to spread religion and to gain control over the newly founded lands. Many explorers travelled to the East in search of a sea route to India. Some of these explorers were:

Christopher Columbus

- Christopher Columbus: In 1492, he sailed west from Europe to find a trade route to India by sea but reached America instead.

- Vasco da Gama: He was a Portuguese explorer and the first European to reach India by sea. His initial voyage to India was the first to link Europe and Asia by an ocean route, connecting the Atlantic and the Indian Oceans. He reached Calicut in 1498.

Vasco da Gama

- Ferdinand Magellan: Between 1519 and 1521, another Portuguese explorer, sailed around the world discovering a passage between the Atlantic and the Pacific Oceans known as the Strait of Magellan. He sailed around the world discovering that the Earth is round.

Ferdinand Magellan

As society evolved, humans began developing wheels which were made of metal and rubber, allowing us to travel quickly and with great comfort. In the 18th century the power of steam was discovered and soon humans learned to power the locomotives of the first trains with the help of steam. Towards the end of 19th century petroleum was discovered from which petrol was extracted and used in cars and small vehicles. Today, petrol and diesel are used to move modern vehicles. The expansion of trade and the curiosity of modern humans to settle down in new places led to the discovery of some modern means of transport.

A replica of the ship in which Ferdinand Magellan travelled the world between 1519–22

Modern Means of Transportation

There are three modes of transportation.

1. Land Transport
2. Water Transport
3. Air Transport

Land Transport

Land transport is a mode of transport in which roads or rail tracks are used for transportation. Humans have been travelling by road for thousands of years. Roadways include carts, cycles, cars, buses, trucks and trains. Among them, the fastest mean of transport is train. Railways has

A train

long been India's transportation backbone. The Indian Railways is the fourth-largest railway network in the world by size.

Did You Know?

The history of Indian Railways dates back to over 160 years ago. On 16th April 1853, the first passenger train ran between Bori Bunder (Mumbai) and Thane, and covered a distance of 34 km.

Water Transport

Water transport is a mode of transport in which boats, ships and sailboats are used for transportation on a sea, ocean, lake, canal or river. Waterways are an important mode of transport for both passenger and cargo traffic in India. It is the cheapest means of transport and is most suitable for carrying heavy and bulky material. It is a fuel-efficient and eco-friendly mode of transport.

A container ship carrying cargo

Air Transport

Air transport is the fastest mode of transportation. It has reduced distances by minimising travel time. It is very essential for a vast country like India, where distances are large and the terrain and climatic conditions are diverse. Air transport in India made a beginning in 1911 over a little distance of 10 km between Allahabad and Naini.

An IndiGo plane

History of Communication

Long before the earliest writings were developed, people communicated with each other by a number of different methods. Early humans could express thoughts and feelings by means of speech or by signs or gestures. They could signal with fire and smoke, drums or whistles.

These early methods of communication were limited to space and time. It was necessary for the people to be present to communicate as they could be used only between persons more or less close to each other. To remove these limitations, writing was developed as a method to communicate.

Hieroglyphs from the tomb of Seti I, earliest form of writing

The earliest form of writing was pictographs – symbols which represented objects – and served to aid in remembering things. These pictographs were impressed onto wet clay which was then dried. Later in time, people developed symbols in writing from the spoken languages.

The Modern Ways of Communication

Sending a message through a pigeon during World War I

Before the invention of the telephone, messenger pigeons were used to dispatch messages. Pigeons are effective as messengers as they have the ability to find their way home over extremely long distances. Pigeons have also been used to great effect in military situations and that is why they are known as war pigeons.

Telegraphs

Telegraph

The telegraph was first invented by Samuel F.B. Morse in 1844. It worked by transmitting electrical signals over a wire laid between stations. Morse developed a code known as Morse Code that assigned a set of dots and dashes to each letter of the English alphabet and allowed for the simple transmission of messages across telegraph lines. Although the telegraph had fallen out of widespread use by the start of the 21st century, it is still used by amateur radio operators.

Telephone

Telephone

A smartphone

The telephone was invented by Alexander Graham Bell in 1876. It brought a revolution in the field of communication. People could talk to any person sitting at a distant place. Though the telephone is still popular, many new developments have taken place in telephonic communication. Now we have mobile phones or cellphones that we carry with us as they are wireless. Smartphones have become quite popular these days which are mobile phones with some advanced features like camera, touch screen, multimedia and internet facility. We can also do all our banking work on a mobile phone. Pictures and videos can also be shared using different apps.

Let's Do

What are some things for which smartphones are useful?

____

Printing Press

Before the printing press was invented, religious texts, books and drawings had to be completed by hand. But with the increase in their demand, it became difficult to prepare them manually in less time. At first, people in China developed a very basic form of printing. It involved letters or images cut on blocks of wood. The block would be dipped in ink and then stamped onto paper.

Around 1430s Johann Gutenberg of Germany, used metal instead of wooden blocks. This was known as a 'movable type machine', since the metal block letters could be moved around to create new words and sentences. With this machine, Gutenberg printed the very first book, the Bible.

A model of the printing press made by Johann Gutenberg

The invention of the printing press made it a lot easier and quicker to produce the copies of books.

Did You Know?

The keyboard invented for the typewriter called 'qwerty', is used today for computers, laptops and smartphones.

Computers

The computer was invented by Charles Babbage in 1822. It is an electronic device that handles or controls information and data. It has the ability to store, retrieve and process data. Computers in recent times have become an integral part of our daily lives. They have improved our efficiency and productivity. In schools, computers can be used to help students in learning the basic concepts better through audios and videos. Computers are very useful in the fields of railways, banking, electricity, telephonic departments, shopping carts, etc. They help doctors in diagnosing diseases in a more accurate manner. They also help in the media and entertainment businesses, as a means of entertainment to the public.

A laptop computer

Man-made Satellites

Man-made satellites are objects placed in space by humans. The first satellite was launched in 1957, named Sputnik 1. Satellites have various uses like sending television signals directly to homes. Satellite-based navigation systems like the Navstar Global Positioning Systems enable anyone to determine his/her location within a few meters. Weather satellites help meteorologists to gather information about different weather conditions across the planet. This helps them to predict the weather conditions.

A satellite

Humans have evolved a lot with time in both physical appearances and lifestyle. This development has given us a great advantage over other animals. Humans have made a great progress in the field of science and technology through education. We should use this technology to make this planet a better place to live.

Points to be Noted

- Early humans started travelling because of various reasons like climate change, for food, hospitable lands for farming, etc.
- The wheel, invented in the Neolithic Age, made it easy to move objects and people.
- Traders and sailors travelled in search of new lands and markets, to spread religion and to gain control over the newly founded lands.
- Modern means of transport are land, water and air transport.
- Early humans could express thoughts and feelings by means of speech or by signs or gestures.
- The earliest form of writing was pictographs – symbols which represented objects.
- Before the advancement of technology, messenger pigeons were used to carry messages or letters to war grounds.
- Various means of communication were invented like telegraphs, telephones, computers and satellites.

Words to Know

Explorer: a person who travels through an unknown place in order to learn about it

Voyage: a long journey involving travel by sea

Locomotives: engines

Eco-friendly: something which is not harmful to the environment

Terrain: a piece of land

Exercises

A. Write T for true and F for false statements.

1. The wheel was invented in the Iron Age. ☐
2. Vasco da Gama was a Portuguese explorer and the first European to reach India by sea. ☐

3. The power of steam was used to move airplanes.
4. Telegraphs were known as the movable type machines.
5. Johann Gutenberg invented the computer.

B. Fill in the blanks.

1. Earlier, humans used to ____________ or ____________ heavy objects to move them from one place to another.
2. The beginning of transportation began with the invention of ____________.
3. The Strait of ____________ is a passage between the Atlantic and the Pacific Oceans.
4. ____________ is the cheapest mode of transport.
5. ____________ is a fuel-efficient and eco-friendly mode of transport.

C. Choose the correct option.

1. Humans could easily settle down in different places using (carts/caves).
2. Christopher Columbus sailed west from Europe to find a trade route to (America/India).
3. (Water/Steam) was used to power locomotives.
4. The Morse Code assigned a set of dots and dashes to each letter of the (English alphabet/Greek alphabet).
5. Weather satellites help (meteorologists/cardiologists) to gather information.

D. Give Reasons

1. People prefer to travel by air across vast distances.
2. The invention of printing press led to the spread of knowledge more quickly and widely.
3. Computers have become an integral part of our lives.

E. Answer the following questions.

1. How did early humans carry heavy objects before the invention of the wheel?
2. Why did early humans start to travel after the invention of the wheel?
3. Name some explorers who travelled to discover the sea route to India.
4. What was the power used to move vehicles in ancient times and how was it different from the power used in ships in the 19th century?

5. How did early humans communicate and what were the limitations that led to the invention of modern means of communication?
6. What are the modern means of communication? Explain any three in detail.

F. Think and Discuss

1. Do you think the world would be as developed as we see it today if the wheel was not invented?
2. Give any five ways in which the Internet can be used. Also discuss about the disadvantages of the Internet.

G. Picture Study

Look at the following emojis and write what they stand for.

________ ________ ________ ________ ________ ________

Life Skills — Spirit of Inquiry

All the inventions that we have read in this chapter came about because some people took the initiative to find out how things can be made which would make our lives more convenient. Whenever we feel that we have an idea to make something work, we should do more research to find out where it leads. You never know what you may end up inventing.

Creative Work

Divide the class into groups and create a telephone using disposable cups and threads.

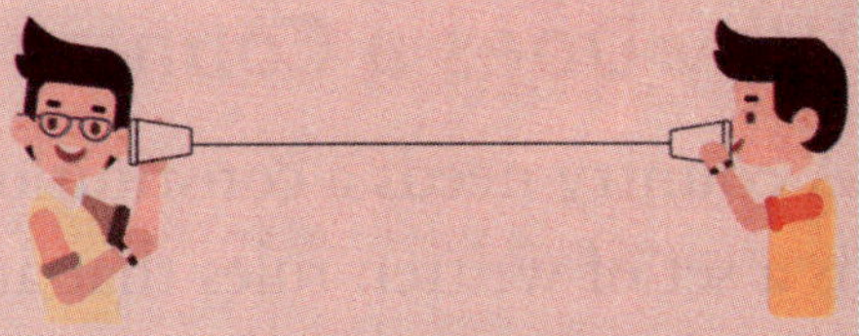

Project Work

Make a timeline marking the inventions that are used today. Also give a detailed account of events that took place when they were invented.

Theme 2: The Constitution of India—Basic Features

4 The Indian Constitution

Warm Up

Answer the following questions.

Do you have to follow certain rules at school? Yes ☐ No ☐

- Write two rules which you have to follow in school.

  1. ______________________________

  2. ______________________________

- What happens when you do not follow these rules?

  1. ______________________________

  2. ______________________________

Your school has a set of rules for students to follow. This is to ensure that there is discipline and orderliness in school, because without it there would be chaos. Similarly, our country also has a set of rules for governments and individual citizens. Just before Independence in 1946, a Constituent Assembly was formed. Its main task was to draw up the constitution for Independent India.

Why Does a Country Need a Constitution?

A country needs a constitution to function well. The constitution of a country is a set of written rules that are accepted by all people living in that country. The constitution is the supreme law that determines the powers and duties of the government and gives certain rights to the people of that nation or state. It ensures that the State's powers are dispersed between different government bodies and individuals, and that the citizens' rights are upheld.

A constitution is necessary for the following reasons:

- First, a constitution tells us what the fundamental nature of our society is.
- Second, it lays down principles and guidelines which are required for people belonging to different ethnic and religious groups to live in harmony.

- Third, it determines the relationship of the citizens with the State.

The Indian Constitution

The Constitution of India is the supreme law of India. This document lays down the procedures, powers and duties of government institutions. It also spells out the Fundamental Rights, Fundamental Duties and the Directive Principles of State Policies.

How Was the Constitution Framed?

A meeting of the Constituent Assembly, 1946

In 1946, a year before independence, a special assembly was constituted which is known as Constituent Assembly. The Constituent Assembly was responsible for drafting a constitution containing laws for the people of independent India. People from all walks of life such as engineers, doctors, lawyers, businessmen, farmers, teachers and many others were part of the Constituent Assembly. A draft committee was formed to finalise the constitution based on the discussions in the Constituent Assembly. Dr B. R. Ambedkar was the chairman of the Drafting Committee. For his role in drafting the Indian Constitution, he is widely considered as the Father of Indian Constitution. It took nearly three years to complete the drafting of Indian Constitution.

Dr B R Ambedkar

First day of Constituent Assembly of India. In the first row (From Left): Dr B. R. Ambedkar, B. G. Kher, Vallabhbhai Patel and K. M. Munshi.

Did You Know?

The original Constitution of India was handwritten by Prem Behari Narain Raizada in a flowly italicized style with beautiful calligraphy. Each page was beautified and decorated by artists from Shantiniketan.

The Indian Constitution was adopted by the Constituent Assembly on 26 November, 1949 and came into force on 26 January, 1950 and this is why, we celebrate this day as Republic Day.

Some important parts of the Indian Constitution are:

- The Preamble
- Fundamental Rights
- The Directive Principles of State Policy
- Fundamental Duties

The Preamble is an introduction to the Constitution. It explains that kind of government that the Constituent Assembly planned for India based on what the people wanted.

Read the Preamble given below and understand the meaning of its keywords.

WE, THE PEOPLE OF INDIA, having solemnly resolved to constitute India into a SOVEREIGN, SOCIALIST, SECULAR, DEMOCRATIC REPUBLIC and to secure to all its citizens:

JUSTICE, social, economic and political;

LIBERTY of thought, expression, belief, faith and worship;

EQUALITY of status and of opportunity; and to promote among them all

FRATERNITY assuring the dignity of the individual and the unity and integrity of the Nation;

IN OUR CONSTITUENT ASSEMBLY this 26th day of November, 1949, do HEREBY ADOPT, ENACT AND GIVE TO OURSELVES THIS CONSTITUTION.

Here is the explanation of the keywords used in the Preamble:

Sovereign	Indian is an independent country. It is free to conduct its own affairs (both internal and external).
Socialist	The wealth of the country should be shared by all Indians. It aims to end poverty, ignorance, disease and inequality of opportunity.
Secular	There is no official religion. Also, all religions are equally important and equally respected. All the citizens of India have the right to profess, practise and propagate the religion of their choice.

Democratic Republic	The government is elected by the people and the head of the country is the president, elected or nominated by the people of the country.
Justice	All the people have access to justice and will be given equal treatment without any social distinction based on caste, colour, race, religion, sex and so on.
Liberty	Everyone has the freedom to speak without fear, to believe in what they like, to practise any religion of their choice without harming anyone's sentiments.
Equality	Equal and fair opportunity to each and every citizen irrespective of their status, class, religion and caste.
Fraternity	To make sure all Indians try to live like brothers and sisters; all people should be treated with respect; the country should remain united, whole and unharmed.

Let's Talk

What role does the Preamble play in our Constitution?

Features of Our Constitution

- The Constitution of India is the lengthiest constitution in the world. It guides or lays down certain instructions on how a country should be governed.
- It defines the structure, procedures and duties of the government.
- The Constitution includes the Fundamental Rights and Duties of the citizens and the Directive Principles which the government must follow to govern well.
- It contains 448 articles in 25 parts, 12 schedules, 5 appendices and 101 amendments as of October 2021.

Constitution of India

Guiding Principles

The ideals of the Preamble are very important for our country to work. To make sure that these are practised by the government institutions, the Constitution has laid down some guidelines. These are called Directive Principles of State Policy. These guidelines help the government to make and implement policies. It is the duty of the State to follow these principles while taking administrative decisions as well as in making the laws. The basic aim of the Directive Principles is to establish a welfare state. The Directive Principles are regarded as the basic foundation of democracy. They are incorporated in the Constitution to meet the economic and social aspirations of the people of our country.

There are several Directive Principles of State Policy. Some are given below.

Children in a school run by the government

- Equal pay should be given to both men and women for equal work.
- People who are old, sick, disabled, unemployed or in any serious need should be provided with help.
- Weaker and backward sections of our society should be helped to improve them educationally and economically.
- Nutrition and public health for Indian citizens should be improved.
- The environment, forests and wildlife of the country should be protected and improved.
- All the objects and monuments of the country should be protected.

Did You Know?

The concept of the Directive Principles (socio-economic rights) were taken from the Constitution of Ireland.

Our Fundamental Rights

India has the second largest population in the world. The citizens of India practise different religions, belong to different castes and speak various languages. In order to maintain peace and harmony in a country with such diversity, our Constitution has given certain rights to all the citizens of India. These rights are known as Fundamental Rights. Fundamental Rights are basic rights which every Indian must have access to.

There are six fundamental rights granted by the Constitution of India.

1. Right to Equality 2. Right to Freedom 3. Right against Exploitation

4. Right to Freedom of Religion 5. Cultural and Educational Rights
6. Right to Constitutional Remedies

Right to Equality

Right to Equality guarantees that all citizens will be treated equal in the eyes of the law. Every citizen, irrespective of his or her caste, class, creed, gender and place of birth, will be given equal opportunity in all fields, such as employment, legal justice, etc.

Right to Freedom

Right to Freedom gives the citizens freedom of speech and the right of expression to express themselves through writing, literature and drama. It also gives them the right to assemble, to move, to reside in a place of their choice or to practise any profession.

Right against Exploitation

Right against Exploitation states that no one can force others to work against their will. If someone is found to be doing so, he/she will be punished by law.

This right also ensures that children below 14 years of age are not forced to work in hazardous conditions where there is a risk to their life and health.

A child working in a factory

Right to Freedom of Religion

The Right to Freedom of Religion gives every Indian the right to follow the religion of one's choice and to propagate it. It also includes the freedom to manage religious affairs and freedom from religious instructions in certain educational institutes.

Cultural and Educational Rights

Cultural and Educational Rights are contained in Articles 29 and 30. This right protects the right of any section of citizens to conserve their culture, language or script.

Right to Constitutional Remedies

The article states that if any citizen is denied any of the Fundamental Rights, then the person has the right to approach the highest court in the land, the Supreme Court for redressal. This means that the Supreme Court is the defender and the guarantor of our Fundamental Rights. This is why Dr B. R. Ambedkar stated that Article 32 is 'the soul of the Constitution and the very heart of it'.

The Constitution of India is dynamic. Additions and deletions can be made to it according to the changing situations. That is why, there are two more rights added to the Constitution.

Right to Information

Under this fundamental right, any citizen of India may request information from a public authority. The main aim of this right is to empower the citizens and to promote transparency and accountability in the working of the Government.

Right to Education

This right has provisions for free and compulsory education for all children between the ages of 6 to 14. Under this right, no child can be held back, expelled or required to pass a board examination until the completion of elementary education.

Children on their way to school

Our Fundamental Duties

Just as our Constitution has provided us some rights, it has given us certain duties to perform. As a citizen of our country, we should be responsible and must perform these duties towards our country. These duties are known as Fundamental Duties.

Our Fundamental Duties are given below:

1. To abide by the Constitution and to respect the national flag and the national anthem
2. To follow the ideals of the freedom struggle
3. To protect the sovereignty and integrity of India
4. To defend the country and render national services when called upon to do so
5. To promote the spirit of harmony and common brotherhood
6. To preserve our composite culture

7. To preserve our natural environment
8. To develop a scientific temper
9. To safeguard public property
10. To strive towards excellence in all spheres of individual and collective activity
11. Parents or guardians to provide opportunities for education to their children between the ages of six to fourteen

These rights and duties have been enshrined in the Constitution keeping in mind the general well-being of the Indian citizens. Hence, we should respect and follow our Constitution.

Let's Do

Write down some occasions when the national anthem is played.

____

Points to be Noted

- A constitution charts out the fundamental nature of a society and the relationship between the citizens and the government.
- A special assembly, known as the Constituent Assembly was set up to draft the Constitution of India.
- Dr B. R. Ambedkar was the chairman of the Drafting Committee and is widely considered as the Father of Indian Constitution.
- The Constitution includes the Fundamental Rights and Fundamental Duties of the citizens and the Directive Principles.
- The Constitution of India contains 448 articles in 25 parts, 12 schedules, 5 appendices and 101 amendments.
- The Directive Principles are the guidelines that should be followed and implemented by the government.
- There are six Fundamental Rights stated in the Constitution.
- These rights are Right to Equality, Right to Freedom, Right against Exploitation, Right to Freedom of Religion, Cultural and Educational Rights and Right to Constitutional Remedies.
- Fundamental Duties should be performed by all the citizens towards the country.

Words to Know

Principle: a rule of conduct based on beliefs of what is right and wrong
Fundamental: the most central and important part of something
Preamble: an introduction to a book or a written document
Procedures: established or official ways of doing something
Propagate: the action of widely spreading and promoting an idea
Culture: the ideas, customs, and social behaviour of a particular people or society
Defender: a person who defends someone or something
Guarantor: a person or thing that gives or acts as a guarantee

Exercises

A. Write T for true and F for false statements.

1. A country needs a constitution to function well. ☐
2. A constitution lays down the principles and guidelines to ensure that people of various groups live in harmony. ☐
3. In India some religions are more important. ☐
4. We should respect our national anthem and national flag. ☐
5. One of the Fundamental Duties is to protect the sovereignty and integrity of India. ☐

B. Fill in the blanks.

1. A special assembly was formed to draft the Indian Constitution which is known as ____________.
2. ____________ is known as the Father of the Constitution.
3. The Constitution of India is the ____________ constitution in the world.
4. The Preamble is an ____________ to the Constitution.
5. Right against Exploitation ensures that children below 14 years of age should not be forced to work in ____________ conditions.
6. ____________ gives people the right to ask for information from a public authority.

C. Choose the correct option.

1. The Constituent Assembly was formed in ____________.

   a. 1947 ☐ b. 1959 ☐

   c. 1967 ☐ d. 1946 ☐

2. Dr B. R. Ambedkar led the ________________.

a. Constituent Assembly ☐ b. Drafting Committee ☐

c. neither a nor b ☐ d. both a and b ☐

3. ________________ were members of the Constituent Assembly.

a. Only rich people ☐

b. Only powerful people ☐

c. People from all walks of life ☐

d. none of the above ☐

4. The Constitution defines the ________________ between the citizens and the State.

a. relationship ☐ b. Directive Principles ☐

c. freedom ☐ d. all of the above ☐

5. In India we have the right to follow ________________ religion/s.

a. one ☐ b. many ☐

c. state ☐ d. none of these ☐

D. Match the following.

Column A	Column B
1. Father of Indian Constitution	a. Liberty
2. Constitution	b. Directive Principles
3. No difference in religion	c. Dr B.R. Ambedkar
4. Welfare state	d. Secular
5. Freedom to speak without fear	e. Supreme law

E. Answer the following questions.

1. What is a constitution?
2. Why is a constitution necessary for a country?
3. What do you understand by the words, Sovereign and Socialist, as stated in the Preamble?
4. Write any two Directive Principles of State Policy.
5. What are Fundamental Rights? How many Fundamental Rights are there in the Constitution?
6. What are Fundamental Duties? Write some Fundamental Duties.

F. Think and Discuss

1. We can elect our own government. Do you think this is an important power that is given to the Indian citizens?
2. Why did Dr B. R. Ambedkar state that Right to Constitutional Remedies is the soul of the Constitution and the very heart of it? Do you agree with him?

G. Picture Study

Look at the pictures and answer the questions that follow.

1. Name the programme shown in the above pictures.

____

2. What is the purpose of this programme?

____

3. Who provides for this programme?

____

Life Skills — Patriotism

We celebrate Independence Day on 15 August. Many people had sacrificed their lives to make India free from the British. They loved their country and because of them we are enjoying the basic rights. We should also love and respect our country. It is our duty to serve the nation and to protect it.

Creative Work

Discuss as a class what Fundamental Duties you can carry out as a child towards the country.

Project Work

Make a chart of 'Rights and Duties' of students in a school (both online and offline). Discuss in the class and display it on the board.

5 Features of a Democratic Form of Government

Warm Up

Answer the following questions.

- Do we choose our leaders in India? Yes ☐ No ☐
- Did people have the authority to choose their rulers in the past? Yes ☐ No ☐

In the earlier chapter we learnt that the Preamble to the Constitution declares India as a democratic country. It is a form of government where the Constitution ascertains Fundamental Rights to all the citizens of the country. Free and fair elections are conducted in a democracy and people can go to court in case of any dispute.

What Is Democracy?

Cleisthenes

The word democracy is taken from the Greek word 'demokratía'. It is made up of two words 'demos' meaning common people and 'kratos' meaning strength. Cleisthenes of Athens, was the first person to introduce the system of democracy in Athens around 508–507 BC. He is also known as the 'The Father of Athenian Democracy'. The democracy that prevailed in Athens was a direct democracy. It had two distinguishing features:

- Any ordinary citizen was selected randomly for administrative and judicial offices, and to a legislative assembly consisting of all Athenian citizens.
- All eligible citizens were allowed to speak and vote in the assembly, which set the laws of the city state.

This democratic form of government began to rise and spread in many parts of the world.

In a democracy the leader is elected by the common people of that country through elections.

The three characteristic features of a democracy are:

- Democracy is a form of government in which the leaders are elected by the people on the principle of one person, one vote.
- Democracy must be based on free and fair elections, where those who are currently in power have a fair chance of losing. Voters should have a choice of candidates
- In a democracy, the final decision-making power rests with those elected by the people.

Did You Know?

India is the largest democratic country in the world.

Types of Democracy

There are two major types of democracies in modern times.

1. Direct Democracy
2. Representative Democracy

Direct Democracy: Direct democracy is also called pure democracy. In this form of democracy citizens participate directly to accept and reject a proposal or a new law. Switzerland is an example of direct democracy where people have more power than the representatives.

Representative Democracy: In this form of democracy few officials are elected to represent a group of people. These officials are elected through a voting system by the citizens of a country. These officials are chosen by the people to make laws for them. India is an example of representative democracy. People elect their representatives in their respective constituencies and these representatives vote to choose the head of the government.

Features of a Democracy

Division of Powers

A very important feature of a democratic government is the division of power into three pillars.

The three pillars of the Indian democracy are the Legislature, the Executive and the Judiciary. The Constitution of India has clearly defined the duties and responsibilities of all three.

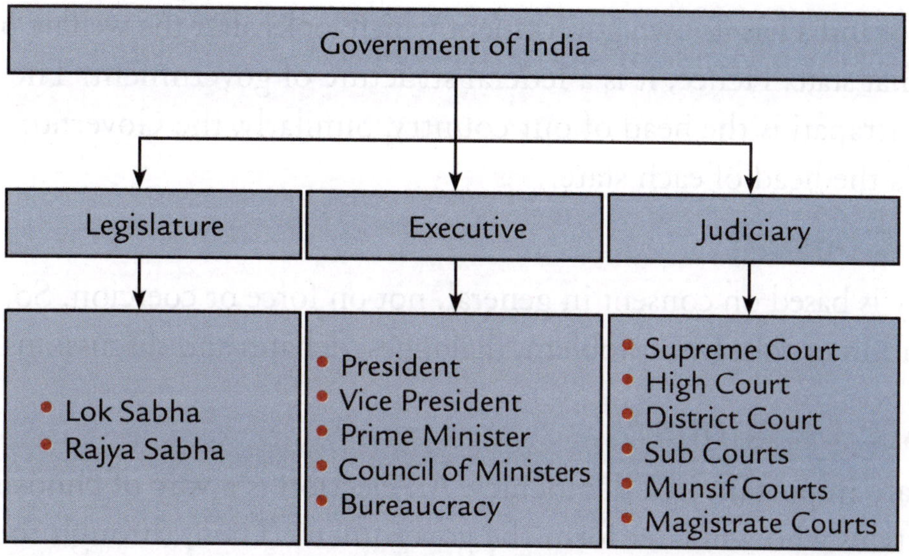

Legislature: This branch is responsible for making the laws to govern the land. They have to be fair and should abide by the Directive Principles of State Policy.

Executive: The executive branch ensures that the laws are properly followed. It also prepares policies which must follow the Directive Principles.

Judiciary: These are the courts. They make sure that laws are properly understood and implemented. People go to the courts to settle their disputes.

System of Checks and Balances

In India the three pillars of power act in such as manner as to keep a check on each other. But a balance is also maintained so that no pillar is more powerful than the other. This is maintained in the following way:

- The judiciary reviews the laws passed by the legislature to see if they have been passed correctly. It also steps in when an action taken by the executive branch is not as per the Constitution.
- The legislatures review the functioning of the executive.
- The executive appoints the judges.
- The legislative branch can remove the judges.

Federal Structure of India

The word federal means a system of government in which the powers of the states of a country and the central or the union government are divided.

The central or union government is the government of the whole country. It looks after the needs, welfare and safety of the people of the country. It has its offices in New Delhi, the capital of India.

Each state of India has its own government which looks after the welfare of the people of that state. Hence, it is a federal structure of government. The President or the Rashtrapati is the head of our country. Similarly, the Governor, or Rajyapal, is the head of each state.

Rule by Consent

Democracy is based on consent in general, not on force or coercion. So, to arrive at any solution or to solve a problem, dialogues, debates and discussions take place.

What Are Elections?

Elections are important in a democracy. An election is a way of choosing representatives who will later form the government. Then, through those representatives, laws and orders are made and maintained in the state. It is a formal decision-making process. Voting is also used in case of a proposal. Our representatives vote in favor or against the proposal.

For an election, the whole country is divided into small parts which are called constituencies. Candidates from these constituencies stand to represent their constituency.

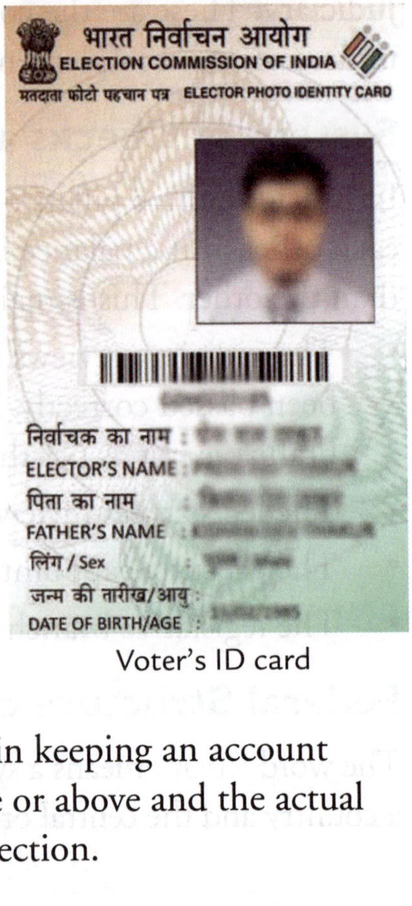

Voter's ID card

The candidate who gets the maximum number of votes, wins the election and becomes the representative of that constituency.

In India, the Election Commission of India is responsible for conducting and supervising elections. The commission makes sure that elections are conducted in a free and fair manner and that each person votes only once. This commission is not under the control of the government and works independently.

The Election Commission registers the voters who are 18 years old or above. These registered citizens are given a Voter ID card. The commission also prepares an electoral roll which has the names of registered candidates printed on it. This electoral roll also helps in keeping an account of the total number of citizens who are 18 years of age or above and the actual number of voters who cast their votes on the day of election.

Not everyone can vote. Voting and choosing a representative is a responsible choice to make. It involves a lot of thinking to take the right decision and mature people have enough wisdom to make the correct choice. So only citizens who are 18 or above have been given the right to vote.

Let's Talk

Why is it important to have a Voter ID card to cast votes?

Earlier, people used to vote by writing the name of the candidate of their choice on a piece of paper. These votes were dropped inside a sealed box known as ballot box. Nowadays schools or government offices are used as polling booths. People are allotted certain places where they have to go and vote. Each booth has an EVM (Electronic Voting Machine) with the names and the party symbols of the candidates. These symbols help the voters who cannot read to recognise the candidate. Voters have to press the button given beside the names and symbols of the candidate. Elections are conducted in secrecy and only one voter at a time is allowed inside the room where the voting machines are kept. This is the called a secret ballot. These machines are enclosed by a screen to maintain privacy.

Ballot Box

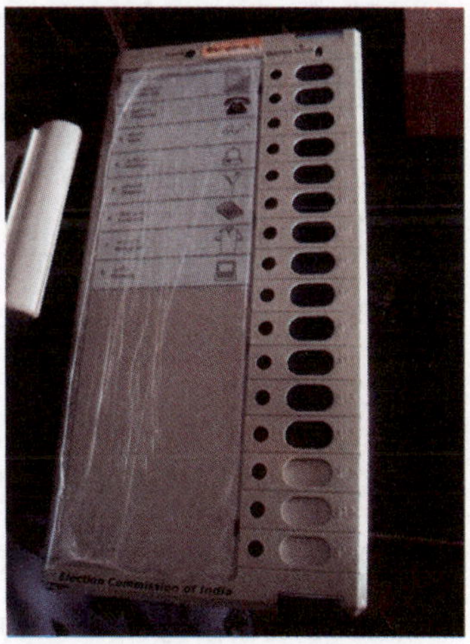

Electonic Voting Machine

The Election Commission counts the votes of the candidates and this is done by using the EVMs. The candidate who gets the maximum number of votes is declared as the winner.

Importance of Elections

Elections are conducted once every five years. This helps the citizens to change the representative or the government in power, in case they are not satisfied with the work done by their representatives or if the promises made by them are not fulfilled. It is the duty of the citizens to keep an eye on the work of the elected candidates to keep them in check. This is the reason why the common people are considered more powerful than the government in a democracy.

Let's Do

- When did the last general elections take place in India?

  ____

- When will the next general elections take place in India?

  ____

Responsibilities of Citizens in a Democratic Polity

Polity refers to an organised society. After gaining independence, our leaders took the tedious task of drafting a Constitution that would give the best of governance to the citizens. In a democracy like India, if the people of the country don't participate in the process, it may threaten the system of democracy.

As citizens we have certain responsibilities in order to keep the process of democracy vibrant. These include:

- Keep ourselves informed about the duties and powers of the government. This will help us speak up in case of any wrong doing.
- It is our duty to vote. Hence, we must exercise this right and choose the deserving candidate during elections.
- Pay taxes honestly, without which the government will not be able to take care of the people.
- Follow the laws because a democracy cannot exist in a lawless society.
- Keep ourselves informed on issues that could have an impact on the country as a whole, for example, the environmental issues.

For the well-functioning of a democratic system, people should participate in the process of elections and should know about their responsibilities as a voter.

Points to be Noted

- In a democracy the leader is elected by the common people of that country through elections.
- Democracy is of two types: direct and representative.

- Some features of democracy are: division of powers, system of checks and balances, federal system and rule by consent.
- An election is a way of choosing representatives who will govern on our behalf.
- People of 18 years of age or above have been given the right to vote.
- Elections are conducted every five years in our country.
- Some duties as citizens are: to keep ourselves informed about the duties and powers of the government, pay taxes honestly, follow the laws and keep ourselves informed on issues that could have an impact on the country as a whole.

Words to Know

Representative: a person who has been chosen on the behalf of a group to represent it

Electoral roll: the list of voters in a particular area

Polling booth: a small area where people go to cast their vote

Ballot: a system of voting

Polity: an organised society, such as a nation or city

Exercises

A. Write T for true and F for false sentences.

1. The word 'Democarcy' is taken from a Latin word. ☐
2. Democracy is a form of government in which the leaders are elected by the people on the principle of one person, one vote. ☐
3. The Constitution of India does not define the duties and responsibilities of the three pillars of power. ☐
4. The executive branch is responsible for making the laws to govern the land. ☐
5. The legislatures review the functioning of the executive branch. ☐
6. The Election Commission of India is responsible for the conduct of elections. ☐

B. Fill in the blanks.

1. Democracy must be based on __________ and __________ elections.
2. Direct democracy is also called __________.
3. An important feature of democracy is the system of __________ and balances.

4. The __________ is the head of our country while the __________ is the head of a state.
5. A list of citizens who are eligible to vote is known as the __________.
6. In a democracy, if the people of the country don't participate in the process, it may __________ the system of democracy.

C. Choose the correct option.

1. In a (representative/direct) democracy, the elected officials represent the people of the constituency.
2. The (executive/legislative) appoints the judges.
3. The (executive/judiciary) branch ensures that the laws are properly followed.
4. In a federal system of government the states (take care/do not take care) of their own affairs.
5. Citizens whose name are registered with the Election Commission are given (a Voter ID card/an Adhaar card).
6. (EVMs/Voter IDs) have the names and the symbols of the candidates.
7. EVMs are hidden behind a screen to make sure that the secrecy of the (votes/machines) are maintained.
8. Elections in India are conducted every (seven/five) years.

D. Match the following.

Column A	Column B
1. Democracy	a. machines that are used to cast and count votes
2. Representative	b. signs to help people identify the party of the candidate
3. Constituency	c. representatives are elected by the people
4. EVMs	d. an area for which someone is elected as the representative
5. Symbols	e. a person who represents a group or a party

E. Answer the following questions.

1. What is democracy? When and where was it first established?
2. What are the types of democracy? Explain in detail.
3. Cite three features of a democracy.
4. What are elections? Why are they important in a democracy?
5. Why do people need to cast their vote?
6. What are the responsibilities of a citizen in a democratic polity?

F. Think and Discuss

1. According to you, which is better–direct democracy or indirect democracy?
2. How can democracy get threatened if we don't participate in the election process?

G. Picture Study

Look at the symbol and answer the questions given below.

NOTA 

1. What is the full form of NOTA? ______________________
2. What does this enable the voter to do? ______________________
3. When was it added as an option in the EVMs in India?

____

Life Skills — Leadership Skills

Every country needs a government to run the country. People have different opinions and ideas. So, it is important to have a government which is ready to listen to people's point of views and work in their favour. Sometimes some major decisions are needed to be taken for the country. A leader should be a good decision maker and should also fulfil the promises he/she makes.

Creative Work

Conduct an election in your class. Make a list of the representatives who are standing in the elections and ask them to choose symbols which will represent them. A couple of students can draw or print the names with the symbols on pieces of paper. Put boxes alongside the names. Distribute the pieces to everyone. The class will tick on the box of the candidate of their choice. The one who gets the maximum number of tick marks is the winner.

Project Work

India is a big country. Every state and union territory has many constituencies. During elections, various parties campaign and represent their candidates and their symbols through flags and posters. Make a list of some of the political parties of India along with the symbols associated with them.

Theme 3: The Earth–Its Geographical Features

6 Locating Places on Earth

Warm Up

Answer the following questions.

- Can you locate your house or school on a map? Yes ☐ No ☐
- How do you tell others where your house is located? ____________________

Just like people use the house or school address or a landmark to tell the location of their house or school, we use lines drawn on maps and globe to locate places on Earth. These lines are called latitudes and longitudes. These lines are not actually found on the planet, but are drawn by cartographers to help us find our way around the curved surface of Earth easier.

Did You Know?

Earth is not a sphere. It is slightly flattened at the North and the South Poles and bulges in the middle.

The Equator

The Equator is an imaginary line that divides the Earth into two equal halves, called the Northern Hemisphere and Southern Hemisphere. The circumference of the Equator is about 40,075 kms long. It is the longest latitude and located at 0°. The temperature near the Equator is hot as the Sun's rays fall straight at the Equator.

Latitudes

The lines that run above and below the Equator are known as latitudes. They form circles like the Equator. As the lines move farther away from the Equator and get closer to the Poles, the circles get smaller. The latitudes can be seen as a dot at the Poles. Latitudes are parallel to each other. The latitudes are numbered as 1° to 90° and are located above and below the Equator. The latitudes at the Poles are numbered as 90°. These numbers are followed by 'N' or 'S' which indicates that the latitudes are either in the Northern or the Southern Hemisphere. A latitude numbered 15° N will be located near to the Equator and lies in the Northern Hemisphere.

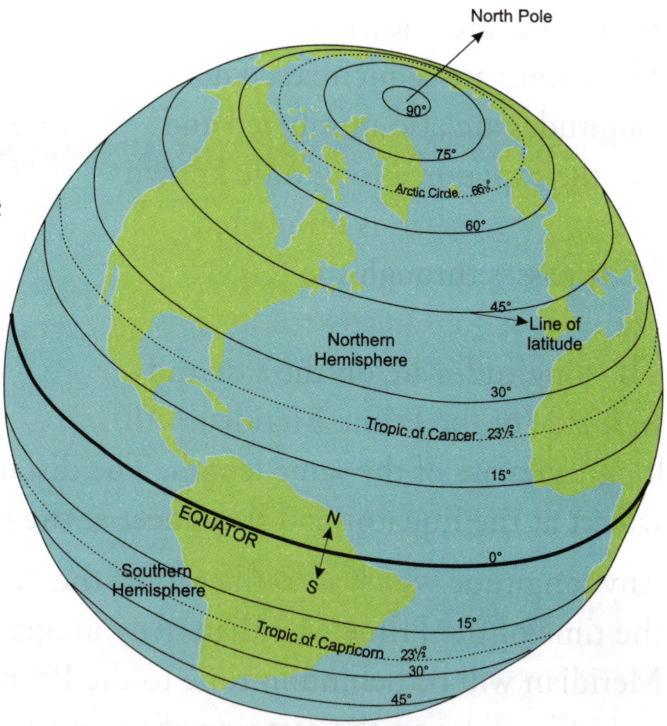

The lines of latitudes

Some important latitudes other than the Equator are:

- **Tropic of Cancer**: This lies in the Northern Hemisphere and is at a distance of 23 ½°N from the Equator.
- **Tropic of Capricorn**: This latitude lies in the Southern Hemisphere and is at a distance of 23 ½°S from the Equator.

Both Tropic of Cancer and Tropic of Capricorn lie at an equal distance from the Equator.

- **The Arctic Circle**: This latitude lies near the North Pole in the Northern Hemisphere at 66 ½°N.
- **The Antarctic Circle**: This latitude lies near the South Pole in the Southern Hemisphere at 66 ½°S.

Did You Know?

There is no permanent human population to the south of the Antarctic Circle.

Let's Talk

Through which states does the Tropic of Cancer pass in India? Talk about it.

Longitudes

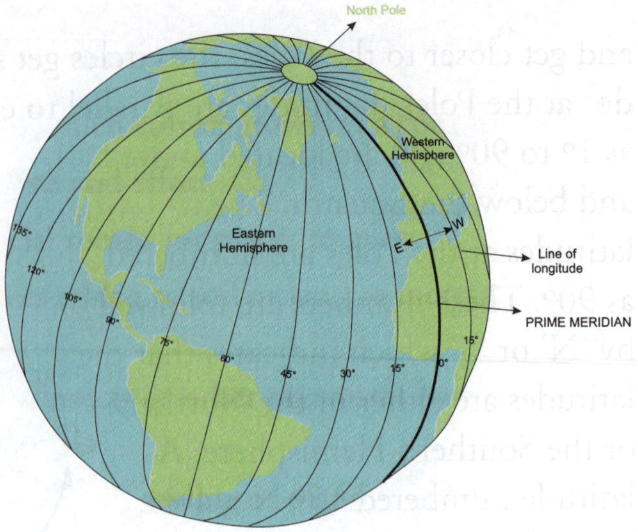

The lines of longitude

The lines that run from North Pole to South Pole are known as longitudes. These lines are semicircles. The longitudes are also numbered and like the Equator, a longitude known as Prime Meridian is numbered 0°. It passes through the Royal Observatory at Greenwich in London. The longitudes are on the east and west side of the Prime Meridian. All longitudes are of the same length. The distance between the longitudes is the widest at the Equator and they meet at the poles.

Any longitude which is to the east of the Prime Meridian will always be ahead of the time of the Prime Meridian. Any longitude which is to the west of the Prime Meridian will be behind in time to the Prime Meridian. A longitude numbered as 15°E will be on the east side of the Prime Meridian and 15°W will be on the west side of it.

The longitudes continue East and West, round the globe, up to 180°.

At 180°, the longitudes from east and west meet, This longitude is known as the 180th Meridian. It is not accompanied by 'E' or 'W'. This longitude is known as the International Date Line. At the Bering Sea, between Asia and North America, the International Date Line bends and goes zig zag. This has been done to make sure that there is only one date in a country. It marks the difference of date between the Eastern and the Western Hemispheres. It is exactly on the opposite side of the Prime Meridian. They both divide the Earth into two equal halves: the Eastern Hemisphere and the Western Hemisphere which lies on the east and west part of the Prime Meridian respectively.

Laser projected from the Royal Observatory in Greenwich, marking the Prime Meridian

Places that fall on the same longitude have the same time.

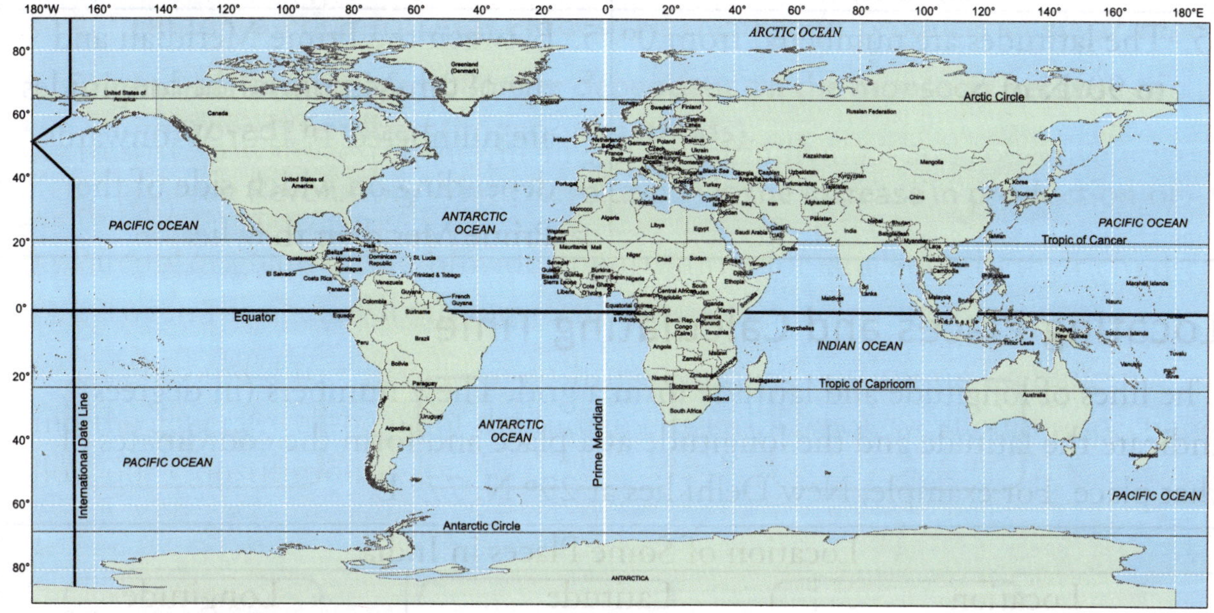

International Date Line

Did You Know?

A.M. stands for Ante Meridiem. It means before noon. P.M. stands for Post Meridiem. It means afternoon.

Difference between Latitudes and Longitudes

Latitudes	Longitudes
1. Latitudes are circles which run parallel above and below the Equator.	1. Longitudes are semi-circles from one pole to the other on both sides of the Prime Meridian.
2. The biggest circle is the Equator which is numbered 0°.	2. The longitude which is numbered as 0° is known as the Prime Meridian.
3. The latitudes are wider near the Equator and get smaller as they move closer to the poles. At each pole the latitude is a dot.	3. Longitudes meet at the pole. They are widest apart at the Equator.
4. Latitudes run in an east-west direction.	4. Longitudes run in a north- south direction.

Latitudes	Longitudes
5. The latitudes are numbered from 0º to 90ºN or S.	5. Between the Prime Meridian and the 180th Meridian, the longitudes are numbered 1º E or W onwards depending on which side of the Prime Meridian they lie.

Locating Places and Calculating Time

The lines of longitude and latitude form a grid. These numbers (in degrees) indicate the latitude and the longitude at a place and form the coordinates of that place. For example, New Delhi lies at 29º N, 77º E.

Location of Some Places in India		
Location	Latitude	Longitude
Abu	27°N	73ºE
Bhopal	23ºN	77ºE
Kerala	11ºN	76ºE
Calicut	11ºN	76º'E
Kolkata	23º'N	88ºE

Location of Some Places in the World		
Location	Latitude	Longitude
Beijing, China	40ºN	116ºE
London, England	51ºN	0º5'W
Sydney, Australia	34ºS	151ºE
São Paulo, Brazil	23ºS	46ºW
Paris, France	49ºN	2ºE

Longitudes help in calculating time

The difference between two consecutive longitudes is of 4 minutes. When we travel eastwards from the Prime Meridian, we need to add 4 minutes on passing each meridian. And when we travel westwards from the Prime Meridian, we need to subtract 4 minutes as we pass each meridian.

Let us look at an example. The current time at the Prime Meridian is 12 noon. Location A is at 4º E longitude and location B is at 4º W longitude. Then, the time at location A will be 12:16 p.m. and time at location B will be 11:44 a.m.

Indian Standard Time is based on the longitude that passes through Naini near Allahabad at 82.5º east of the Greenwich Mean Time.

Let's DO

Calculate the time difference between the Indian Standard Time and the Greenwich Mean Time.

GMT: 0° IST: 82.5°

The time difference: ______________________

Points to be Noted

- The lines drawn on maps and globes are imaginary lines. These lines are called longitudes and latitudes.
- The Equator divides the Earth into two halves: Northern Hemisphere and Southern Hemisphere.
- The lines that run above and below the Equator are known as latitudes. They form circles like the Equator. Latitudes are parallel to each other.
- Tropic of Cancer, Tropic of Capricorn, Arctic and Antarctic Circle are some important latitudes.
- The lines that run from North Pole to South Pole are known as longitudes.
- The longitude at 0° is known as Prime Meridian and the longitude at 180° is the International Date Line.
- All longitudes and latitudes are numbered.
- Longitudes are used to calculate time.

Words to Know

Cartographers: persons who draw or produce maps
Hemisphere: half of a sphere
Meridian: a line that is drawn on a map from North Pole to South Pole
Grid: a network of lines that cross each other
Coordinates: numbers or letters that are used to tell the fixed position of a place

Exercises

A. Write T for true and F for false sentences.

1. The Equator is the shortest latitude. ☐
2. The Tropic of Cancer lies in the Southern Hemisphere. ☐
3. The latitudes can be seen as a dot at the poles. ☐
4. The longitudes are widest apart at the poles. ☐
5. A longitude numbered as 44°E will be on the east side of the Prime Meridian. ☐

6. Latitudes meet at the poles.
7. Coordinates are the points which indicate the location of a place.

B. Fill in the blanks.

1. __________ and __________ are known as imaginary lines.
2. __________ used latitudes and longitudes to locate a point on Earth.
3. 35°N indicates that the latitude is in the __________ Hemisphere.
4. The Antarctic Circle is numbered as __________ and it lies in the __________ Hemisphere.
5. __________ meet at the poles.
6. Meridian at 180° is known as the __________.
7. Longitudes are __________ at the Equator.

C. Choose the correct option.

1. The lines that run above and below the Equator are known as (longitudes/latitudes).
2. Both the Tropic of Cancer and the Tropic of Capricorn lie at (equal/unequal) distance from the Equator.
3. The Arctic Circle lies in the (Northern/Southern) Hemisphere.
4. The (Prime Meridian/International Date Line) passes through the Royal Observatory at Greenwich in London.
5. The Prime Meridian and the International Date Line divide the Earth into (two/three) equal halves.
6. (Coordinates/Grids) help in finding the location of a fixed point.

D. Answer in one word.

1. People who draw maps __________
2. Latitude at 0° __________
3. Latitude at 66 ½° N __________
4. Meridian at 180° __________
5. Meridian at 0° __________
6. A network of lines __________

E. Answer the following questions.

1. What is the Equator? Why are the regions near the Equator hot?
2. Which are latitudes? Explain them in detail.
3. Give a brief account on the important latitudes.
4. What are longitudes? Explain them in detail.
5. What is the Prime Meridian? What is its use?
6. What is the difference between latitudes and longitudes?

F. Think and Discuss

1. Nowadays we have smartphones which help us to find directions and places through the GPS. How did people in ancient times travel from one place to another?
2. What kind of climate would the regions between the tropics and the circles on both sides of the Equator have? Why?

G. Picture Study

Look at the map. Write the names of the continents through which the following latitudes pass.

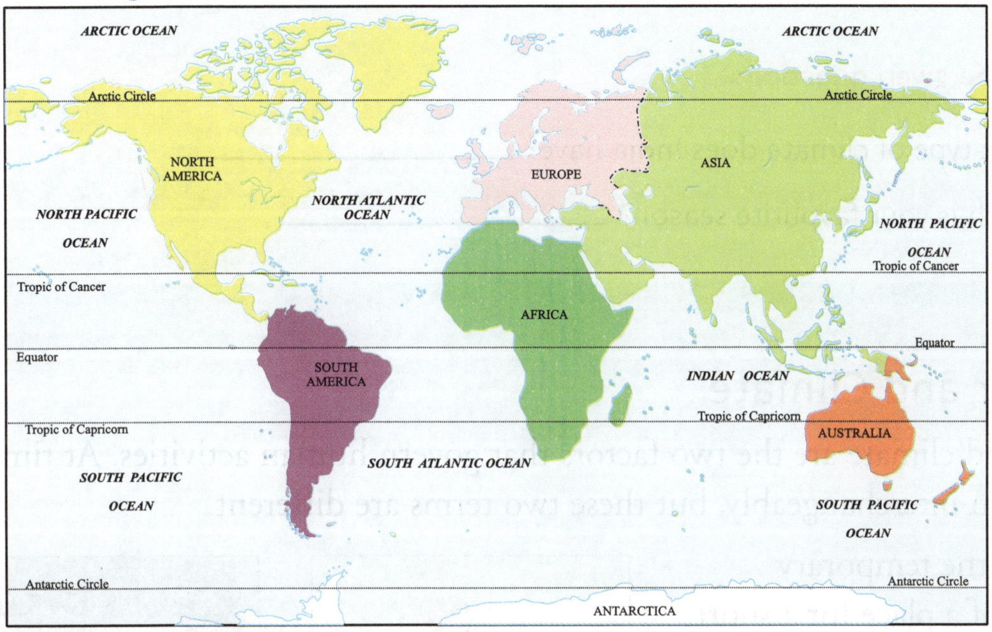

Map not to scale

1. Tropic of Cancer ______________________
2. Tropic of Capricorn ______________________
3. Arctic Circle ______________________
4. Antarctic Circle ______________________

Life Skill — Critical Thinking

Draw a grid pattern over the map of your school compound. Then give the exact location of the playground, auditorium and your classroom.

Creative Work

Make a model of a globe and cover it with a grid of latitudes and longitudes. Also mention the important latitudes and longitudes.

Project Work

Find out what horse latitudes are. Also find out how they got the name?

7 Weather and Climate

Warm Up

Answer the given questions.

- What type of climate does India have? ____________________
- Which is your favourite season? ____________________

Weather and Climate

Weather and climate are the two factors that govern human activities. At times we use them interchangeably, but these two terms are different.

Weather is the temporary condition of a place for a short period of time. Sometimes we wake up to a sunny morning but in the afternoon, clouds spread over the place and it begins to rain. This is because the atmosphere of that place changes over a short time. These changes which happen over a short period of time are called weather.

Sunny

Rainy

Windy

Cloudy

When the weather takes a regular pattern for over a long period of time it becomes the climate of that place.

In Antarctica the weather is always cold. So, Antarctica has a cold and dry climate.

At places where the summers are hot and moisture remains in the atmosphere, the climate of that place is hot and wet. Places where summers are windy or cool and winters are cold have a pleasant climate.

Weather of a place changes in a short period of time while the climate of a place does not change for hundreds of years.

Did You Know?

In the equatorial region, the weather is more or less hot and wet throughout the whole year.

Factors that Affect the Climate of a Place

The climate of a place depends upon the geography of a place. This includes different factors like latitude or distance from the Equator, altitude or height of a place, distance from the sea and direction of wind.

Latitude or Distance from the Equator

In the earlier chapter, we read that places which are near the Equatorial regions are hot. This is because the rays of the Sun fall directly over the Equator. The nearer a place is to the Equator the hotter or warmer it will be. As we move away from the Equator, places get cooler. This is because as we move away the sunrays do not fall directly on that place. Mogadishu is very close to the Equator while Stockholm is far from the Equator. In January, Mogadishu has hot temperature with 30° C while Stockholm has a frigid temperature of –5°C.

Let's DO

Name a few places which fall on the Equator. Also, mention the summer and winter temperatures of those places.

1. ______________________________

2. ______________________________

3. ______________________________

Altitude or Height of a Place

Mountains are colder than the plains

Altitude is the height of the place above the sea level. Sea level is taken as the parameter for measuring the altitude of a place. Mountains and plateaus are cooler than the places which are at sea level. This is because mountains are above the sea level. Even if the high lands are near the Equator, they are always cold and covered with ice at the top. The places at low altitudes are hot because the air at lower level or close to the Earth absorb more heat than the air which is at higher level. Kashmir which is at a high altitude is colder than Delhi which is at a lower altitude and is hot.

Distance from the Sea

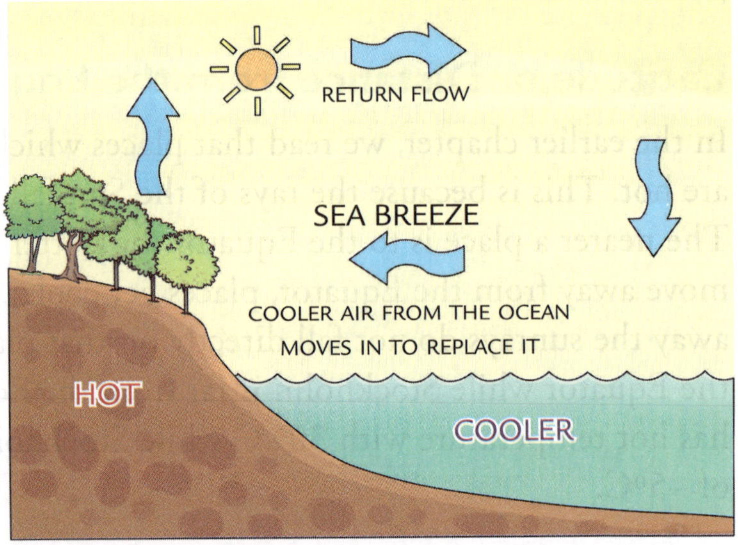

The distance from the sea determines the climate of a place. Places near the sea have moderate climate but places away from the sea are very cold in winter and hot in summer. This is because land gets heated faster and loses heat faster than water. During summer, the land gets heated quickly and the air above the land surface becomes hot. This hot air rises up and the cool air above the sea blows towards the land and occupies the space that is created. The cool air brings down the temperature of that place which makes it cool. The places which are far away from the sea remain hot because there is no cool air to bring the temperature down.

During winter, the land cools down more quickly than the water in the sea. The warm air above the sea moves towards the land and raises the temperature of that place and makes it warm. But the places which are far from the sea do not get the same warm air because by that time the air reaches those places, it loses its warmth. Hence, they remain cold in winter. Bhopal is far from sea and remains hotter in summer and cooler in winter than Goa which is near the coast. Another example is Hyderabad which is hotter in summer and cooler in winter as compared to Visakhapatnam which is on the coast.

Places near the sea are humid because the air present near the coast have a lot of water vapour in it. High humidity makes the atmosphere uncomfortable as perspiration does not dry easily. Andaman and Nicobar Islands are near the Equator and the climate there is hot and humid.

Let's Talk

What could be some of the problems faced by people living in the coastal areas?

Direction of Wind

Horizontal moving air is called wind. The direction of the winds that blow regularly at a particular time of the year has an effect on the climate. Hot winds increase the temperature of a place while cold winds decrease the temperature of that place. The winds also bring rain with them. For example, the monsoon winds that blow over the Indian subcontinent are also seasonal winds. The south-west monsoon winds bring rain from June to September and the north-east monsoon winds bring rain during December and January.

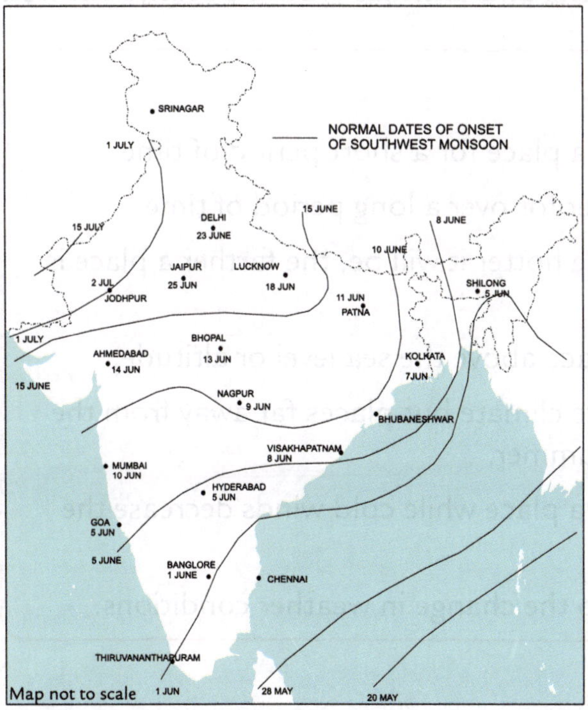

Direction of south-west monsoon winds

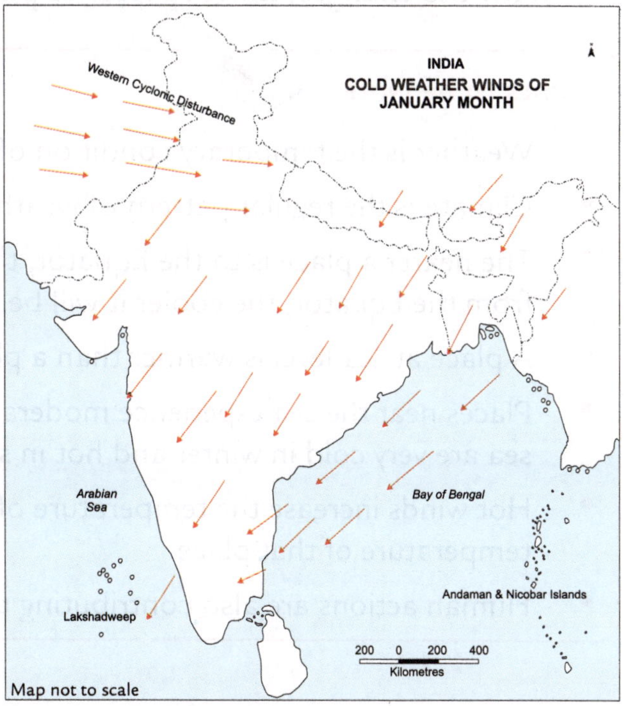

Direction of north-east monsoon winds

Change Due to Human Actions

In addition to the factors listed above, human actions also contribute to it. In earlier times, the impact of human actions on the climate was negligible. But of late, our actions are impacting it in a big way. Technological advancement has made it possible for us to set up massive factories. Big industries and increased means of transport results in excessive burning of fossil fuels. With the increase in population, large forests areas have been felled to make way for human habitation. All these actions have led to the rise in the carbon dioxide levels. This has resulted in more greenhouse gases being released into the atmosphere. Carbon dioxide, methane, nitrous oxide and chlorofluorocarbons (CFCs) are examples of greenhouse gases. These gases trap heat in the atmosphere, keeping the Earth's surface warmer than it would be if they were not present.

Effects of Climatic Change

If the Earth keeps getting warmer, these are the likely consequences:

- The ice caps and glaciers at the poles will melt faster. This would lead to a rise in the sea level, thereby affecting the coastal areas.
- We will experience more of extreme weather, that is hotter summers and colder winters. We will also experience more droughts.
- With the changes, more species of plants and animals would become extinct.

Points to be Noted

- Weather is the temporary condition of a place for a short period of time.
- Climate is the regular pattern of weather for over a long period of time.
- The nearer a place is to the Equator, the hotter it will be, the farther a place is from the Equator, the cooler it will be.
- A place at sea level is warmer than a place above the sea level or altitude.
- Places near the sea experience moderate climate but places far away from the sea are very cold in winter and hot in summer.
- Hot winds increase the temperature of a place while cold winds decrease the temperature of that place.
- Human actions are also contributing to the change in weather conditions.

Words to Know

Pleasant: nice or satisfying

Parameter: a limit or boundary which defines the scope of a particular process

Absorbs: takes in or soaks up

Humidity: a quantity representing the amount of water vapour in the atmosphere or in a gas

Perspiration: sweating

Subcontinent: a large distinguishable part of a continent

Exercises

A. Write T for true or F for false statements.

1. The weather of a place changes over a long period of time. ☐
2. The climate of a place does not depend on its altitude from the sea level. ☐
3. Water heats up faster and cools down faster than land. ☐
4. Places that are nearer to the Equator are cooler. ☐
5. High humidity makes the atmosphere comfortable. ☐
6. The south-west monsoon winds bring rain from June to September. ☐
7. When the ice caps melt faster, the sea level would go down. ☐

B. Fill in the blanks.

1. Climate is the regular pattern of __________ for over a long period of time.
2. The climate of a place depends upon the __________ of a place.
3. __________ is taken as the parameter for measuring the altitude of a place.
4. High __________ makes the atmosphere uncomfortable.
5. Horizontal moving air is called __________.
6. Greenhouse gases __________ heat in the atmosphere, keeping the Earth's surface warmer.

C. Choose the correct option.

1. Places where summers are cool and winters are cold have a (pleasant/ humid) climate.
2. The land (reflects/absorbs) more heat at low altitude.
3. The distance from (the sea/space) determines the climate of a place.
4. The warm air above the sea moves towards the land and (increases/ decreases) the temperature of a place.
5. Places near the coast are humid because a lot of (water vapour/dust) is present in the air.
6. The wind also brings (snow/rain) with them.
7. With the rise in sea level, more species of plants and animals would (survive/perish).

D. Match the following.

Column A	Column B
1. A place near to the Equator	a. horizontal moving air
2. Altitude	b. bring rain with them
3. Winds	c. weather
4. A condition for a short period of time	d. hot
5. Monsoon winds	e. height of a place above sea level

E. Answer the following questions.

1. What is weather? How is it different from climate?
2. Enlist the factors that affect the climate of a place.
3. How does altitude have an effect on the climate of a place?
4. How does the distance of a place from the sea affect the climate of a place?
5. How do winds affect the climate of a place?
6. How have human actions contributed to changes in the climate?

F. Think and Discuss

1. How do weather and climate affect human activities?
2. People usually go to mountains or highlands with their families during summer vacations. Why?

G. Picture Study

Look at the pictures and answer the given questions.

A. 

B. 

1. What type of climate does picture A have? ____________________
2. What type of climate does picture B have? ____________________

Life Skills — Critical Thinking

What kind of food and clothes would people living near the coastal areas eat and wear? Would the people living in cold places be having the same food and would they be wearing the same kind of clothes? Does the climate of a place impact our way of life? Discuss as a class.

Creative Work

Divide the class into four groups and equally divide the states of India among those groups. Ask each group to collect information on the climate of those states and then compare them to find the hottest and the coldest states of India.

Project Work

Do a study of the weather of the place where you live and keep a record of the day-to-day changes.

8 Solar and Lunar Eclipse

Warm Up

Do this activity in class.

The teacher will choose one student to be the Sun.

- That 'Sun' will stand in a spot designated by the teacher. Then the teacher will draw an oval around the 'Sun'.
- The teacher will choose another student to be Earth. That student will go around the 'Sun'. While going around the 'Sun', the 'Earth' would also spin slowly.

What the two students have demonstrated to the class are the two movements of the Earth: rotation and revolution.

The rotation and revolution of celestial bodies around one another is a natural phenomenon. This rotation and revolution sometimes causes other natural phenomena such as formation of eclipses.

In ancient times, people used to worship the Sun as it was the main source of heat and light. But sometimes when people saw that the light of the Sun was partly or completely hidden, they thought it to be the wrath of God and were frightened by it. Later scientists and astronomers studied this phenomenon of nature and termed it as eclipse.

What Is an Eclipse?

The word, eclipse has been taken from the Greek word 'eklepsis' which means darkening of a heavenly body. An eclipse takes place when one heavenly body such as a Moon or a planet moves into the shadow of another heavenly body.

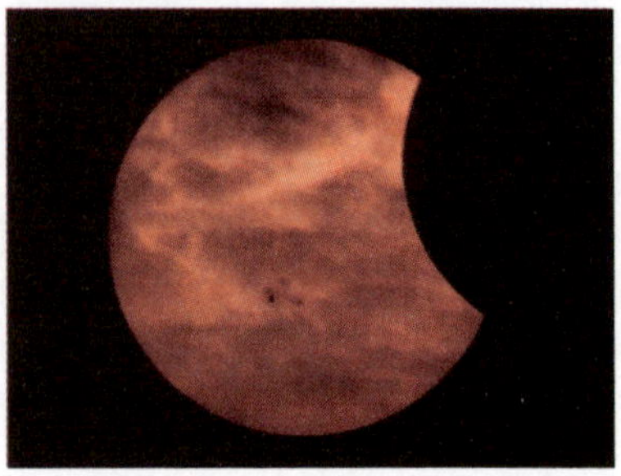

Partial solar eclipse

Eclipses take place for the following reasons.

- The movement of Earth around the Sun.
- The movement of the Moon around the Earth.

There are times when the Sun, Earth and the Moon fall in a straight line on account of their movement. At such positions, a shadow formed by sunlight falls on either the Moon or the Sun as seen from the Earth. This is an eclipse.

Parts of a Shadow

Total solar eclipse

A shadow has three parts: umbra, penumbra and antumbra. The umbra is the innermost and darkest part of a shadow, where the source of light is completely blocked by the obstructing body. An observer within the umbra experiences a total eclipse.

The penumbra is the region in which only a portion of the light source is blocked by the obstructing body. An observer in the penumbra experiences a partial eclipse.

The area of shadow beyond the point of umbra is called antumbra. In an antumbra the outline of one object can be seen from behind the other. The object which is in the shadow area appears to be entirely contained within the disc of the light source.

Solar Eclipse

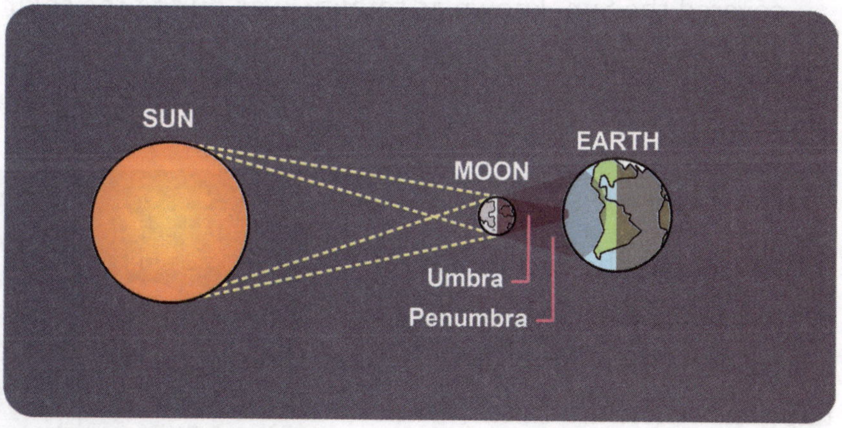

Solar eclipse is the eclipse of the Sun. A solar eclipse takes place when the Sun is partly or completely hidden. While orbiting the Earth, the Moon comes in between the Sun and the Earth. It blocks the light of the Sun from reaching the Earth and its shadow falls on the Earth. A solar eclipse can be partial or total. During a solar eclipse, the Moon casts two shadows on Earth. The first shadow is called the umbra. As you can see, it is the dark centre of the Moon's shadow. It gets smaller as it reaches the surface of the Earth. The second shadow is called penumbra. It is the larger shadow that falls on the Earth (look at the diagram given).

Solar eclipses are of two types. One is the total solar eclipse during which the Sun is completely hidden.

This happens when the Moon comes between the Sun and Earth and casts the darkest part of its shadow, the umbra, on Earth. The people in the umbra region see a total solar eclipse. The sky becomes dark like night sky. For a total solar eclipse to occur, the Sun, the Moon and the Earth should be in straight line.

When the penumbra part of the Moon's shadow falls on the Earth, it gets bigger as it reaches the Earth. People in the penumbra see a partial solar eclipse. For a partial solar eclipse the three bodies do not need to be in the straight line.

Solar eclipses are amazing phenomena which nature provides us with. They lasts for only a few minutes. But we should never look directly at a solar eclipse as it can temporarily or permanently damage our eyes. There is a special equipment that is used to view solar eclipses.

Let's Talk

Why do solar eclipses last only for a few minutes?

Did You Know?

Till date, the longest measured duration in which the Moon completely covered the Sun, known as totality, was during the solar eclipse of July 22, 2009 over India, Nepal, Bhutan and China.

Lunar Eclipse

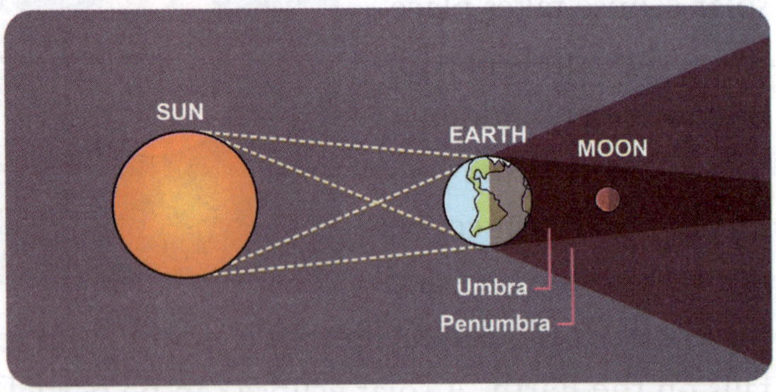

'Luna' means the Moon. Lunar eclipse takes place when the Moon is hidden from view. This happens when the Earth, while orbiting around the Sun comes in between the Moon and the Sun. Then, the shadow of the Earth falls on the Moon as the Earth blocks the light of the Sun from reaching the Moon.

Total lunar eclipse

In a total lunar eclipse, the Sun, Moon and Earth are in a straight line, with the Sun and the Moon on opposite sides of the Earth. The Moon looks reddish during a total lunar eclipse. In a partial lunar eclipse, only a small portion or fraction of the Moon comes into the Earth's shadow. Lunar eclipses lasts for a few hours and people can watch them directly without any protective covering for the eyes.

Partial lunar eclipse

Let's DO

Find out when the last lunar and solar eclipses occurred in India.

____

Points to be Noted

- When one heavenly body moves into the shadow of another heavenly body, an eclipse occurs.
- An eclipse is a phenomena in which one celestial body casts a shadow on another celestial body.
- A shadow has three parts: umbra, penumbra and antumbra.
- A solar eclipse occurs when the Moon comes in between the Sun and the Earth.
- A lunar eclipse occurs when the Earth comes in between the Sun and the Moon.

Words to Know

Phenomena: an observable fact or event

Astronomer: a scientist who studies the objects in the sky, including planets, galaxies, black holes and stars

Opaque: objects which do not allow light to pass through them

Exercises

A. Write T for true and F for false statements.

1. The word, eclipse, means light. ☐
2. The orbit of the Earth around the Sun is not the reason for the occurrence of eclipses. ☐
3. There are five types of eclipses. ☐
4. Umbra is the darkest part of the shadow. ☐
5. When the penumbra part of the Moon's shadow falls on the Earth, it gets bigger as it reaches the Earth. ☐

B. Fill in the blanks.

1. An ____________ takes place when one heavenly body moves into the shadow of another heavenly body.

2. A solar eclipse takes place when the __________ is partly or completely hidden.
3. We should never look directly at a __________.
4. Only a small portion or fraction of the Moon comes into the Earth's shadow in a __________ eclipse.
5. Lunar eclipses last for __________.

C. Choose the correct option.

1. In ancient times, people were (happy/frightened) by the occurrence of eclipses.
2. A shadow is formed when sunlight falls on a (transparent/opaque) object.
3. A total solar eclipse occurs when the (umbra/penumbra) part of the Moon's shadow falls on Earth.
4. People standing in the (penumbra/antumbra) see a partial solar eclipse.
5. During a (solar/lunar) eclipse, the Sun and the Moon are on opposite sides of the Earth.

D. Who Am I?

1. I am a phoenomena in which one body comes in front of another and casts a shadow. __________
2. I am the darkest part of a shadow. __________
3. I am formed beyond the point of umbra. __________
4. For me to occur, the Sun, the Moon and the Earth should be in a straight line. __________
5. I come between the Sun and the Moon during lunar eclipse. __________

E. Answer the following questions.

1. What is an eclipse?
2. What is a shadow and what are the three parts of a shadow?
3. When does solar eclipse occur?
4. Name the two shadows cast by the Moon on the Earth during a solar eclipse.
5. What is lunar eclipse? Explain in detail.

F. Think and Discuss

Why can one look at a lunar eclipse without any protection to the eyes but use a protective equipment while looking at a solar eclipse?

G. Picture Study

Look at the picture and answer the given questions.

1. What does this image show?

____

2. When did the longest solar eclipse occur?

____

3. What happens during this phenomena?

____

Life Skills — Developing a Scientific Temper

Some people believe that one must not eat or drink during an eclipse as it could do harm to the body. Is this based on science or is it just a superstition? When we are in doubt about any such practise or belief we should always try to find out the logic behind it.

Creative Work

Do the following activity in groups of five to understand how solar and lunar eclipses take place.

Materials Required:

- One Meter Stick
- One 3.5 cm Clay Ball
- One 1 cm Clay Ball
- Three Toothpicks
- Two Binders

What to do:

1. Attach a binder clip to the 1 cm mark on the meter stick.
2. Attach the other binder clip to the 100 cm mark on the meter stick.
3. Stick 2 toothpicks into the 3.5 cm clay ball and attach it to one binder clip.
4. Stick the last toothpick into the 1 cm clay ball and attach it to the other binder clip.
5. Go outside with the model and stand under the Sun to see strong shadows.
6. Tilt your meter stick so the 3.5 cm clay ball (Earth) faces downward, to model a solar eclipse.
7. Flip the meter stick so the 1 cm ball (Moon) faces towards the ground, to model a lunar eclipse.

Project Work

Find out what happens to tides during a lunar eclipse. Record your observations in your notebook.

9 Major Temperature Zones of the Earth

Warm Up

In chapter 6 we learnt about some important latitudes. Can you name them? Also write the degrees of these latitudes.

____

____

____

____

____

These latitudes divide the Earth into three temperature zones. These zones help in determining the climate of a place.

Temperature Zones

The temperature zones are also known as heat zones. The zone which falls near the Equator is usually hot, while those that are a little away from the Equator have a moderate climate. The places which are near the poles have a cold climate. The Sun plays a major role in determining the climate of a region. The climate in these temperature zones also affects the vegetation as well as the lifestyle.

The three temperature zones are:

- The Torrid Zone
- The Temperate Zone
- The Frigid Zone

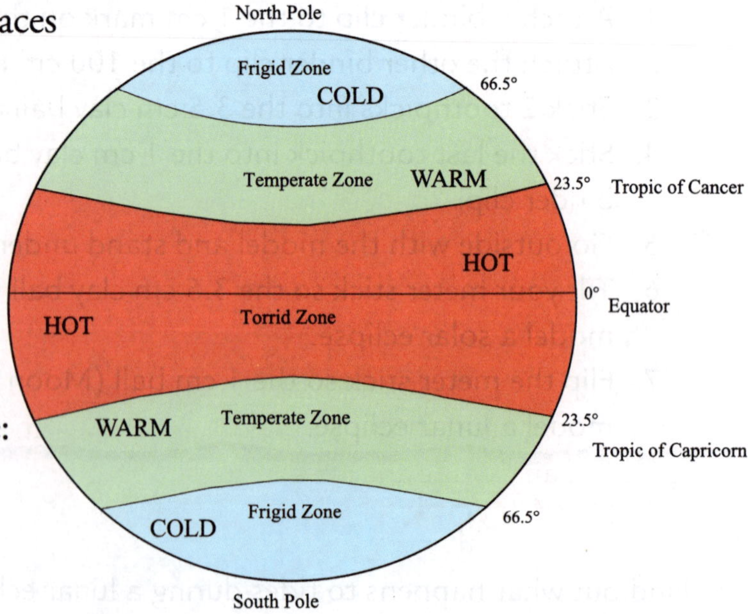

The three heat zones of the Earth

The Torrid Zone

Torrid means 'very hot'. The Torrid Zone is the hottest of all three zones. The zone between the Equator and the Tropic of Cancer (23 ½° N) and the Tropic of Capricorn (23 ½° S) form this region.

The Equator passes through this zone and the areas 10° N and 10° S to the Equator form the equatorial region. The areas beyond 10° right up to the tropics on both sides form the tropical regions.

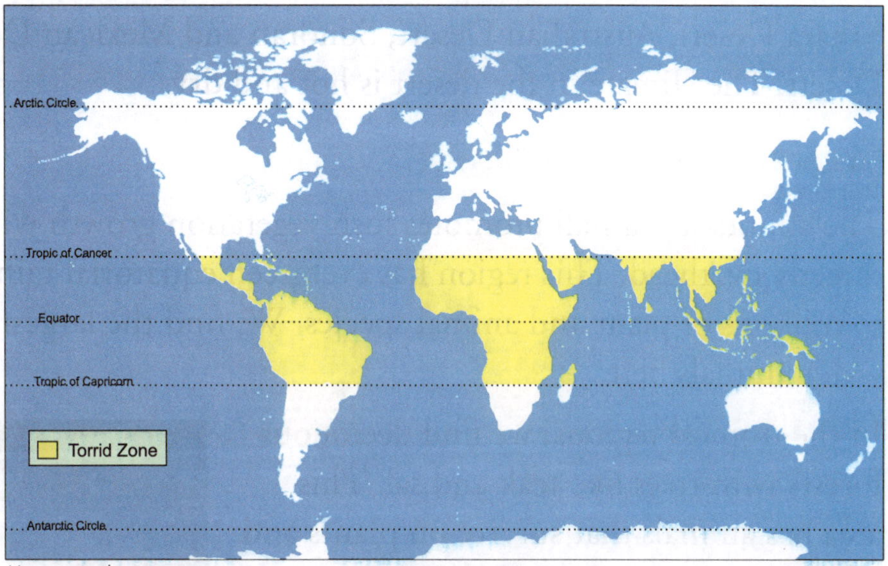

The Torrid Zone

The Torrid Zone has an extreme climate. It is home to both the world's densest rainforests like the Amazon Forest and driest deserts like the Sahara Desert.

Climate

Some of the areas that are considered to be the hottest places on Earth can be found in this region.

Parts of Africa, South America and South-East Asia fall in the equatorial region. This region experiences hot and humid condition. The region on either side of the Equator experiences daily rainfall. The heat causes a lot of evaporation leading to clouds building up over that area. By late afternoon, when it cools off a bit, the water vapour condenses and falls as rain in the evening. These showers are known as 4 o'clock showers. The temperature stays relatively uniform from day to night. There is no winter in this region as sunlight falls directly on these areas all round the year.

Did You Know?

The water of seas in the tropics is warm due to which violent hurricanes, cyclones and typhoons arise in tropical regions.

The intense heat of the Sun falling on the Equator causes air currents that help in the formation of clouds over Equatorial regions, which then cause rains and thunderstorms.

Some parts of South-East Asia and the Indian subcontinent falls in this tropical region.

This climate in this region is characterised by hot summers and rainy seasons. The winters are cool in the plateaus and hills. The hot deserts in this zone are the Sahara Desert, Australian Desert, Sonoran and Mexican Desert and the Arabian Desert. The climate in the desert is hot and dry.

Vegetation and Wildlife

The abundant rainfall promotes lush vegetation growth with the aid of the Sun directly overhead. This region has evergreen equatorial rainforests which is home to millions of plant and animal species. We find the largest species of land and water animals here.

In the tropical regions, we find deciduous forests with trees like teak and sal. This area has animals that survive on plants and other animals.

A beetle found in the Amazon rainforest

In the desert region, the vegetation that exists are plants with thick stems, deep roots and thorny leaves. Some animals found here are camels, lizards and snakes.

A Madagascar moth, the biggest moth in the world

The equatorial region is sparsely populated with indigenous people or tribals. There are more people inhabiting the tropical regions.

Some of the animals found in this region range from tiny insects, like beetles and moths, to large mammals, like gorillas and elephants.

Amazon Rainforest

Elephant

The Temperate Zone

Temperate means 'neither too hot nor too cold'. This zone lies between the Tropic of Cancer and Arctic in the north and the Tropic of Capricorn and Antarctica in the south. The Midwest region of the US, southern Canada and central Europe in the Northern Hemisphere and Chile, Uruguay, New Zealand, South Africa and southern part of Australia in the Southern Hemisphere come in the Temperate Zone where they are located at the lower latitudes. The Temperate Zones have dry and arid regions as well as moist coasts. Places where there is adequate amount of precipitation promote the growth of grasses which forms grasslands in this zone.

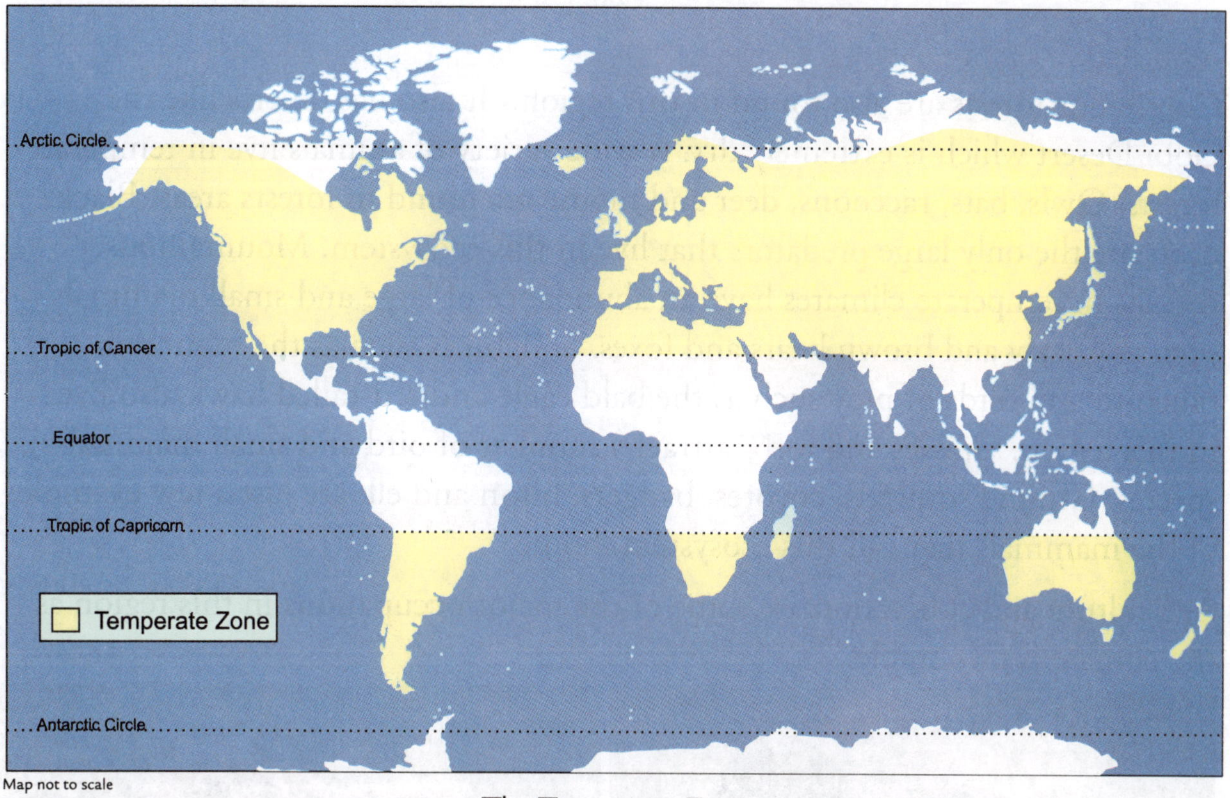

The Temperate Zone

Climate

The Temperate Zone has a moderate climate. The areas which are close to the tropics are warmer and the places which are closer to poles are cold. The winters are cold but relatively mild and summers are warm, wet and stormy. Most places in the Temperate Zone experience four distinct seasons—spring, summer, autumn and winter.

Vegetation and Wildlife

The temperature and rainfall in the region impact the vegetation. We find grasslands in the Temperate Zone. In areas where there is not enough regular rainfall to support the growth of a forest, but not so little that a desert forms, grasslands are found. In fact, grasslands often lie between forests and deserts.

They are known by different names in different regions. In North America they are known as Prairies, Steppes in Europe and Asia, Savannahs and Velds in Africa, Rangelands in Australia and Pampas in South America. The Prairies are called the 'Wheat Basket of the World'.

Did You Know?

Grasslands are found in every continent except Antarctica.

Coniferous forests are also found in this region. It also has deserts like the Gobi Desert which is extremely dry. A wide variety of animals live in temperate forests. Owls, bats, raccoons, deer and moose are found in forests areas. Black bears are the only large predators that live in this ecosystem. Mountainous regions in temperate climates have an abundance of large and small mammals such as grizzly and brown bears and foxes. Songbirds such as the mountain bluebird and birds of prey such as the bald eagle and red-tailed hawk also live in this region. Grasses and forbs attract a number of bird and small mammal species. Ground squirrels, coyotes, badgers, bison and elk are just a few examples of the mammals that call this ecosystem, home.

Agriculture and cultivation are some of the major occupations in this region as the climate is favourable.

Bison

Brown bear

Let's DO

Where are coniferous forests found in India?

____

The Frigid Zone

Frigid means 'frozen'. This zone lies between the North Pole and the Arctic Circle in the north and between the Antarctic Circle and the South Pole in the south. The northern parts of Canada, Scandinavia, Russia and Alaska, Greenland and the Arctic Ocean form the Frigid Zone in the Northern Hemisphere. The Southern Frigid Zone comprises the Antarctica, and the southern parts of Chile, Argentina and New Zealand. Antarctica is the coldest continent and is always frozen and therefore known as the Frozen Continent. These Frigid Zones are also known as polar ice caps.

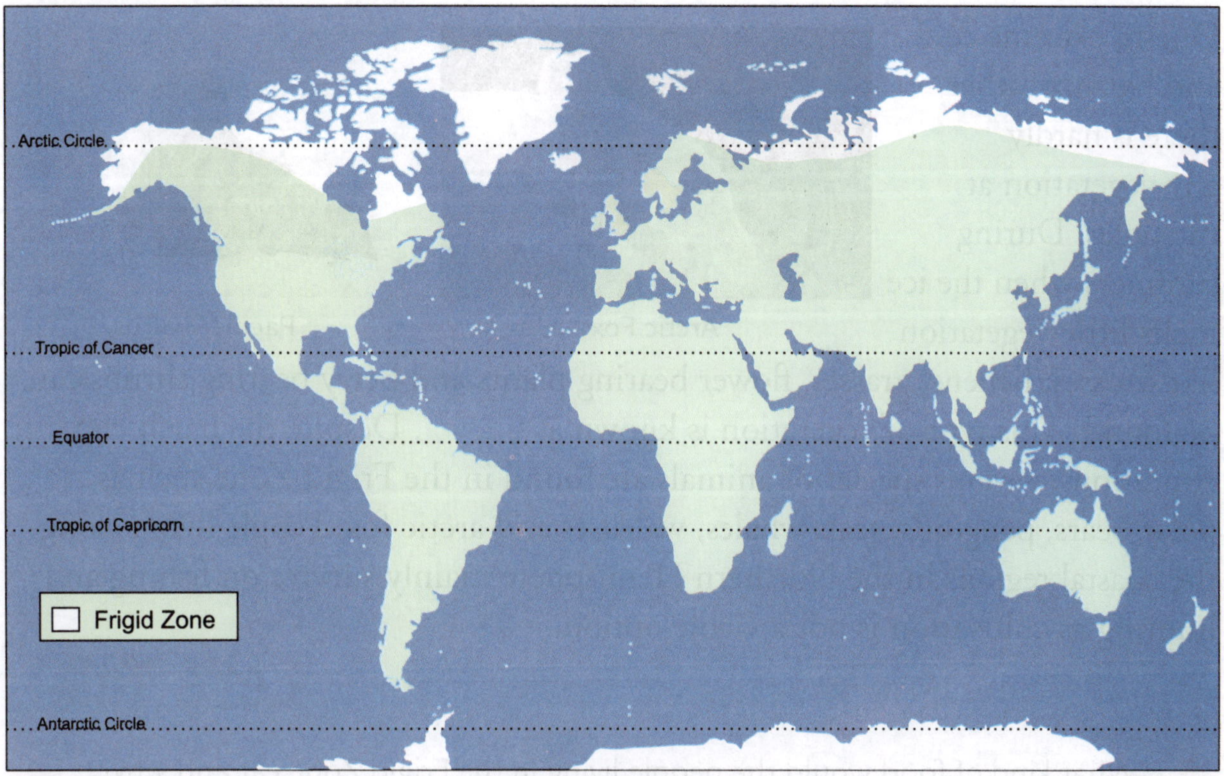

Map not to scale

The Frigid Zone

Climate

Antarctica ice caps

Antarctica pearlwort

This climate is characterised by a long season of severe winter and even the summer season is cold. These regions are known for blizzards. At the poles, there is continuous darkness for six months during winters and in summer, there is continuous light for weeks. This is due to the revolution of the Earth. When the North Pole has summer, the South Pole will have winter and vice-versa.

Did You Know?

Polar lights (aurora polaris) are a natural phenomenon found in both the northern and southern polar regions that can be truly awe inspiring. Northern lights are also called by their scientific name, aurora borealis, and southern lights are called aurora australis.

Vegetation and Wildlife

Arctic Fox

Pacific Walrus

Due to extreme cold and harsh weather there is hardly any vegetation at the poles. During summers when the ice melts little vegetation like mosses, lichens, grasses, flower bearing plants and berry bearing shrubs can be found. This type of vegetation is known as tundra. Despite the harsh climatic conditions, various species of animals are found in the Frigid Zone such as polar bears, penguins, seals whales, walruses and arctic fox. People living along the coastal regions in the Northern Hemisphere mainly survive on fishing and hunting as cultivation is not a viable option.

Let's Talk

What kind of food would the people living in the Frigid Zone eat and why? Discuss.

Effects of Human Activity on Temperature Zones

Orangutan

For years human beings have used nature for their own survival. Sometimes they do this by damaging the natural environment. This has an adverse effect on animal and plant life as well as the climate.

In the Temperate Zone people have converted grasslands into farming lands for agriculture purposes. In some regions towns and cities have been developed. These activities have led to the decrease in the number of the Bison of North America. In the Torrid Zone, forests have been cut down to make space for housing or agriculture and to collect wood like timber. This has led to the disappearance of orangutan. The local tribes living in these forests have lost their traditional way of life.

The large ice caps of Antarctica are melting due to human activities like deforestation and excessive emission of CFCs and carbon dioxide. This has led to an increase in the temperature of the Earth known as global warming.

Points to be Noted

- The latitudes divide the Earth into three temperature zones.
- The climate in these temperature zones also affects the vegetation as well as lifestyle of humans and animals living there.
- Torrid Zone is the area between the Equator and the Tropic of Cancer and Tropic of Capricorn.
- Temperate Zone lies between the Tropic of Cancer and Arctic Circle in the north and Tropic of Capricorn and Antarctica Circle in the south.
- Frigid Zone lies between the North Pole and the Arctic Circle in the north and between the Antarctic Circle and the South Pole in the south.
- Human activities have an adverse effect on animal and plant life as well as on the climate.
- Deforestation and excessive emission of CFCs and carbon dioxide have led to an increase in the temperature of the Earth.

Words to Know

Moderate: in the middle, not too high not too low

Vegetation: plants in a particular area

Ecosystem: a place or environment shared by all the living things, from plants and animals to microscopic organisms

Precipitation: changing of water vapours into liquid or solid

Deciduous: trees that shed their leaves once a year

Coniferous: evergreen trees and shrubs having usually needle-shaped or scale-like leaves

Predators: animals that naturally hunt or kill other animals

Forbs: herbaceous flowering plants other than grass

Blizzards: severe snowstorms with high winds

Deforestation: cutting down of trees

Exercises

A. Write T for true and F for false statements.

1. The heat zone which is a little away from the Equator has a moderate climate. ☐

2. The Sun plays a major role in determining the climate of a region.
3. The Torrid Zone has a pleasant climate.
4. The Midwest region of the US, southern Canada and central Europe come in the Temperate Zone.
5. The Frigid Zone contains areas that are some of the hottest places on Earth.
6. At the poles there is continuous darkness for six months.

B. Fill in the blanks.

1. The Equator passes through the ____________.
2. The ____________ deserts lie in the Torrid Zone.
3. The summers in Temperate Zone are ____________, ____________ and ____________.
4. In ____________ Zone when the North Pole has summer, the South Pole will have winter.
5. The vegetation in Frigid Zone is known as ____________.
6. The increase in Earth's temperature is known as ____________.
7. The cutting of trees is known as ____________.

C. Choose the correct option.

1. The (latitudes/longitudes) divide the Earth into three temperature zones.
2. The climate in the Torrid Zone is generally hot and (humid/dry).
3. The winters in the Temperate Zone are cool with (mild/hot) summers.
4. The Temperate Zones experience (four distinct seasons/no season).
5. (Coniferous/Deciduous) forests are found in the Temperate Zone.
6. Polar bears are found in the (Torrid/Frigid) Zone.

D. Answer the following in one or two words.

1. The temperature zones are also known as this: ____________
2. The important imaginery line that passes through the Torrid Zone: ____________
3. The number of seasons experienced in the Temperate Zone: ____________
4. Another name for grasslands found in Asia: ____________
5. The type of vegetation found in the Frigid Zone: ____________

E. Answer the following questions.

1. Name the three temperature zones of the Earth.

2. Why is there abundant vegetation growth in the Torrid Zone?
3. Explain what kind of climate and vegetation and wildlife is found in the Temperate Zone.
4. Why do people living in the Frigid Zone hunt animals instead of practising agriculture?
5. Explain how human interference has an adverse impact on the climate and wildlife of a place.

F. Think and Discuss

1. Why are the prairies called the 'Wheat Basket of the World'? Does this mean this region is good for agriculture?
2. Imagine you are one of the indigenous people of the Torrid Zone. You are totally dependent on the forest for survival. One day a businessman comes and asks you to leave the land. What will you do in such a situation? Now keeping this in mind, discuss how tribal people have suffered for years in the name of development.

G. Picture Study

Look at the picture and answer the questions that follow.

1. In which zone are these animals found? ______________
2. Where does this zone lie? ______________
3. Is it easy to live in this zone? ______________
4. How do humans survive in this zone? ______________

Life Skills — Being Adaptable

People adapt themselves to the prevailing surroundings to survive. Similarly, we should learn to adapt to our surroundings and the changes happening around us. This will help us to make the best of the situation and we will not feel left behind.

Creative Work

Divide the class into three groups and do a research work on Amazon Rainforest, Sahara Desert and Antarctica. Then, make a PowerPoint presentation to represent what you have discovered through your research.

Project Work

Make a list of the countries that fall under the various heat zones and the main occupation in these countries.

10 Location of India and Neighbouring Countries

Warm Up

Answer the following questions.

- Where do you live? ____________
- Who lives in your neighbourhood? ____________
- Are your neighbours friendly? ____________

India is officially known as the Republic of India. It is also known as Bharat and Hindustan. New Delhi is the capital. India is a secular country and is home to millions of people from different religions. India is a developing country and one of the fastest developing economies of the world.

Location and Size

India is located in the southeast of Asia, the largest continent in the world. India is the second most populated country in the world with a population of 1.2, billion people. It is also the seventh largest country in the world by area.

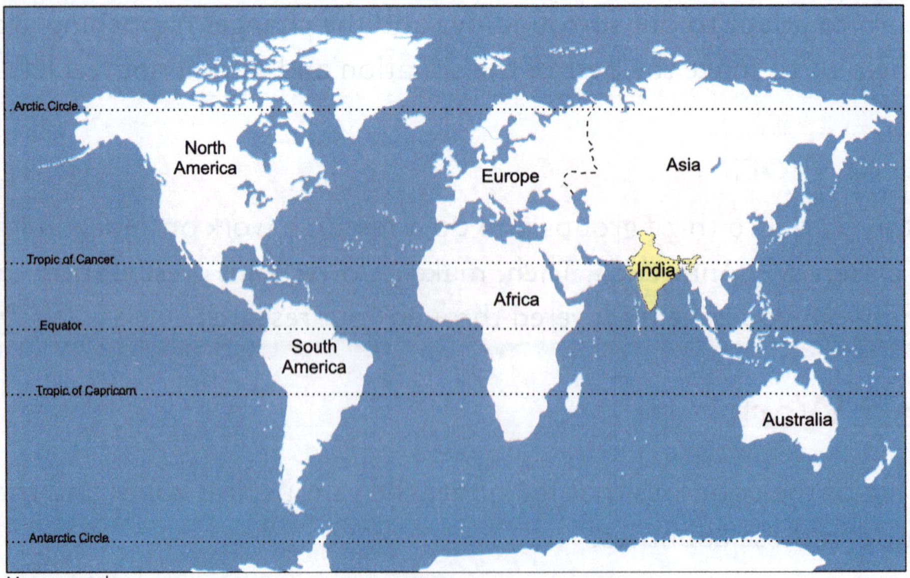

Map not to scale

Location of India in the world

It lies in the Northern Hemisphere between 8°4'N and 37°6'N and longitudes 68°7'E and 97°25'E. The Tropic of Cancer passes through eight Indian states–Gujarat, Rajasthan, Madhya Pradesh, Chhattisgarh, Jharkhand, West Bengal, Tripura and Mizoram. It stretches from Jammu and Kashmir in the north to the Andaman and Nicobar Islands in the south and from Gujarat in the west to Arunachal Pradesh in the east.

India is a peninsula. A peninsula is a land which is covered by water bodies on three sides. India is surrounded by the Arabian Sea in the west, the Indian Ocean in the south and the Bay of Bengal in the east.

Political Divisions of India

India is a vast country with people belonging to different cultures and traditions. For this reason, the country is divided into 28 states and 8 union territories. These states have their own government to administer the needs of the people and the growth of the states. The largest state is Rajasthan and the smallest is Goa. Every state has its own language and culture. India has two island groups: the Andaman and Nicobar Islands in the east in the Bay of Bengal and the Lakshadweep Isands in the Arabian Sea in the west.

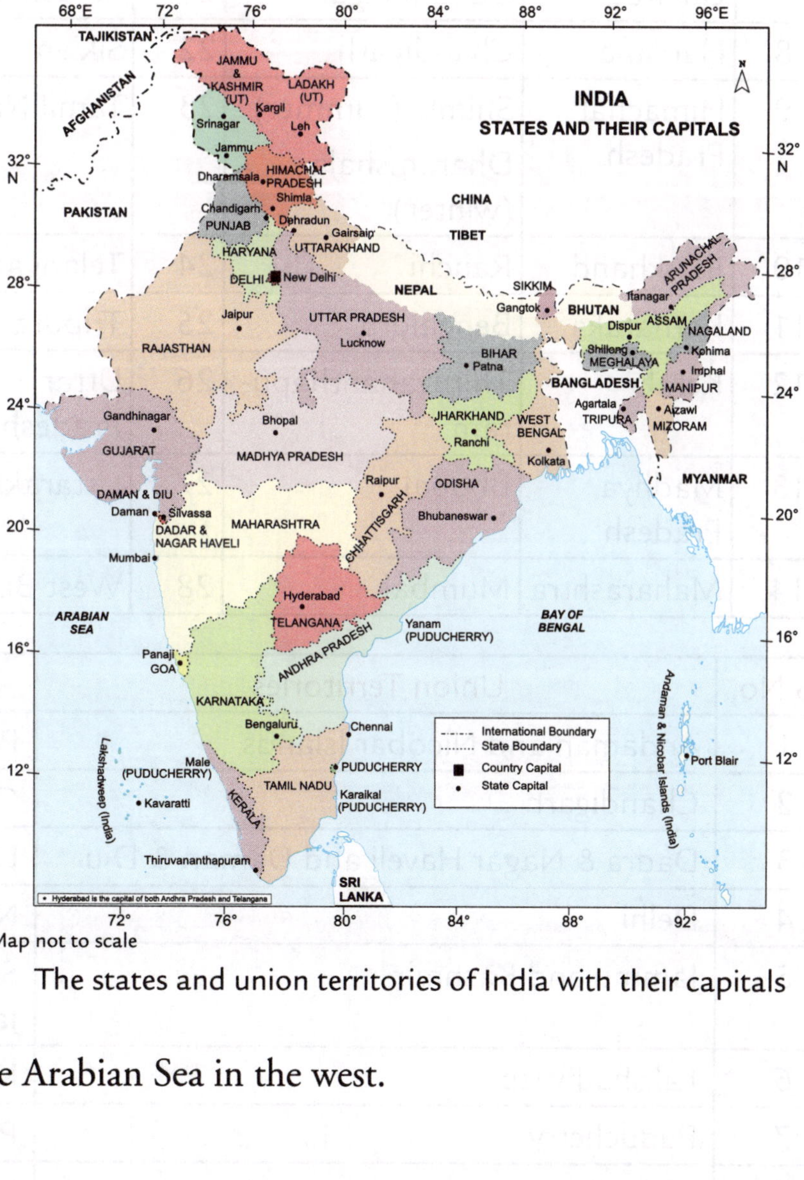

Map not to scale

The states and union territories of India with their capitals

Given below is the list of states and union territories with their capitals.

S.No	State	Capital	S.No	State	Capital
1	Andhra Pradesh	Amaravati	15	Manipur	Imphal
2	Arunachal Pradesh	Itanagar	16	Meghalaya	Shillong
3	Assam	Dispur	17	Mizoram	Aizawl
4	Bihar	Patna	18	Nagaland	Kohima
5	Chhattisgarh	Raipur	19	Odisha	Bhubaneswar
6	Goa	Panaji	20	Punjab	Chandigarh
7	Gujarat	Gandhinagar	21	Rajasthan	Jaipur
8	Haryana	Chandigarh	22	Sikkim	Gangtok
9	Himachal Pradesh	Shimla (summer) Dharamshala (winter)	23	Tamil Nadu	Chennai
10	Jharkhand	Ranchi	24	Telangana	Hyderabad
11	Karnataka	Bengaluru	25	Tripura	Agartala
12	Kerala	Thiruvananthapu-ram	26	Uttar Pradesh	Lucknow
13	Madhya Pradesh	Bhopal	27	Uttarakhand	Dehradun (winter) Gairsain (summer)
14	Maharashtra	Mumbai	28	West Bengal	Kolkata

S.No.	Union Territories	Capital
1	Andaman and Nicobar Islands	Port Blair
2	Chandigarh	Chandigarh
3	Dadra & Nagar Haveli and Daman & Diu	Daman
4	Delhi	New Delhi
5	Jammu and Kashmir	Srinagar (summer) Jammu (winter)
6	Lakshadweep	Kavaratti
7	Puducherry	Pondicherry
8	Ladakh	Leh and Kargil

Did You Know?

The union territories of Daman and Diu, Dadra and Nagar Haveli were merged as a single union territory on January 26, 2020.

Physical Divisions of India

The physical divisions tell us about the land features of a country. India has varied land features. In the north you can see the high mountains, hills and valleys, then we have plains and plateaus. These land features are called its physical features. India is divided into six main physical divisions.

1. The Himalayas or the Northern Mountains
2. The Northern Plains
3. The Great Indian Desert
4. The Peninsular Plateau
5. The Coastal Plains
6. The Island Groups

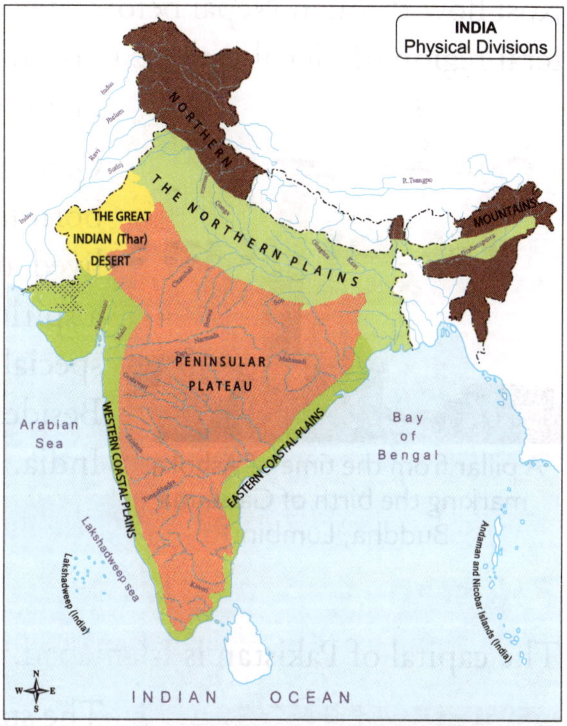

Map not to scale

The physical divisions in India

India's Neighbours

Just as we have neighbours, India also has many neighbouring countries. They are all a part of Asia and most of them are in the Indian subcontinent. India shares its boundaries with China, Bhutan, Nepal, Pakistan and Afghanistan in the north or north-west, and with Bangladesh and Myanmar in the east. India also shares water borders with Sri Lanka in the south. India is a member of SAARC (South Asian Association for Regional Cooperation). This organisation was formed to encourage cooperation and friendly relationship amongst the member countries.

Let's DO

In which physical division of India does your state lie? Write it here.

____

Federal Democratic Republic of Nepal

The capital of the Federal Democratic Republic of Nepal or Nepal is Kathmandu.

Flag of Nepal

Five states of India share their borders with Nepal. They are Uttarakhand, Uttar Pradesh, Bihar, West Bengal and Sikkim. We also share the Himalayan ranges. Rivers like Kosi flow through Nepal before they enter India. The terai region of Nepal is the extension of the Gangetic Plains of India.

A pillar from the time of Ashoka, marking the birth of Gautama Buddha, Lumbini

Gautama Buddha, the founder of Buddhism, was born in Lumbini, in Nepal. When he grew up, he lived and preached his ideas in India. So, we share a spiritual bonding. The Indian army also has a special regiment named the Gorkha Regiment. Besides, we have Nepalese working and living in India.

Pakistan

The capital of Pakistan is Islamabad.

Flag of Pakistan

Mohenjo-Daro

The states of Punjab, Rajasthan, Gujarat and the union territory of Jammu and Kashmir and Ladakh share their borders with Pakistan. We share the high mountain ranges in the north. The Northern Plain region of India extends to Pakistan. The Thar Desert also spills into Pakistan. The Indus River and its five tributaries flow from India to Pakistan.

Before 1947, India and Pakistan were one nation. So, many monuments which form a significant part of India's history are located in Pakistan. The ruins of the twin cities of Harappa and Mohenjo-Daro, of the Indus Valley Civilisation, the ruins of Taxila University, one of the earliest universities in the world, are in Pakistan.

Harappa

China

Flag of China

The capital of China is Beijing.

Arunachal Pradesh, Himachal Pradesh, Sikkim and Ladakh share their borders with China. The Himalayas create a boundary between the two countries.

Tsang Po River

The river Tsang Po originates in China and flows into Arunachal Pradesh.

Fa-Hien visited India during the time of the Guptas and Hiuen Tsang visited India during the reign of Harshavardhana. These were Buddhists monks who travelled to India in search of Buddhists texts and have left their accounts of India during their stay here. There was trading between China and India since early times, as well.

Bhutan

Flag of Bhutan

The capital of Bhutan is Thimpu.

Paro Taktsang, where Padmasambhava is said to have meditated

Bhutan shares its border with Arunachal Pradesh, Sikkim, Assam and West Bengal. Bhutan is situated in the Himalayas, the natural boundary of India.

Buddhism, the main religion, was introduced to Bhutan by a saint, Padmasambhava from India.

Republic of the Union of Myanmar

Flag of Myanmar

The capital of Myanmar is Naypyidaw.

The four North-East states of Arunachal Pradesh, Nagaland, Mizoram and Manipur share their borders with Myanmar.

Myanmar on the left and India on the right bank of Tio River

During the times of the British, Myanmar was a part of India, and was governed from Kolkata. Besides, the two countries have had trading relations since ancient times. That is how Buddhism was introduced in Myanmar.

Did You Know?

The India–Myanmar border has a Free Movement Regime (FMR) which allows tribes living along the border to travel 16 km across either side of the border without visa restrictions.

Bangladesh

Flag of Bangladesh

The capital of Bangladesh is Dhaka.

West Bengal, Assam, Tripura, Mizoram and Meghalaya share their borders with Bangladesh. The rivers Ganga and Brahmaputra flow through India into Bangladesh. The delta formed by these two rivers, the Sundarbans, spread across the two countries.

During the British rule, Bangladesh was a part of India. In 1947, India got divided into India and Pakistan. Pakistan comprised West Pakistan and East Pakistan, which was Bangladesh. In 1971, Bangladesh was freed of Pakistan.

Let's Talk

What are some of the things that are shared by India and Bangladesh besides the geographical features?

Sri Lanka

Flag of Sri Lanka

The capital of Sri Lanka is Sri Jayawardenepura Kotte.

We don't share a land boundary with this country unlike our other neighbours. The two countries are separated by the Palk Strait.

India has always maintained relations with Sri Lanka since around the 4th century BC with the introduction of Buddhism by the children of Emperor Ashoka, Mahindra and Sanghamitra.

Points to be Noted

- India is a secular country and it is a multilingual society.
- India is located in the southeast of Asia.
- India is a peninsula, which means it is covered by water bodies on three sides.
- India is divided into 28 states and 8 union territories which have their separate governments.
- The physical divisions tell us about the land features of a country.
- India shares its land boundaries with seven countries.
- Besides sharing land borders, India also shares historical connections with all the neighbours.

Words to Know

Secular: not connected with any religious or spiritual matters
Multilingual: using or speaking several languages
Continent: a very large area of land
Administer: to manage an organisation
Subcontinent: a large distinguishable part of a continent
Strait: a narrow area of water that connects two larger areas of water

Exercises

A. Write T for true and F for false sentences.

1. India is one of the fastest developing economies of the world. ☐
2. India lies in the Northern Hemisphere. ☐
3. Imphal is the capital of Meghalaya. ☐
4. India is divided into six main physical divisions. ☐
5. India shares its border with Thailand. ☐
6. Emperor Ashoka himself spread Buddhism in Sri Lanka. ☐

B. Fill in the blanks.

1. India is officially known as ____________.
2. India is a ____________ country and it is a ____________ society.
3. ____________ is the largest and ____________ is the smallest state of India.
4. India has the ____________ Islands in the Arabian Sea in the west.
6. The land features of a country are known as ____________.
7. India shares its ____________ region with Nepal.
8. Myanmar was a part of India during the ____________.

C. Choose the correct option.

1. India is the (seventh/tenth) largest country in the world by area.
2. India is surrounded by the (Arabian Sea/Bay of Bengal) in the west.
3. India is divided into (nine/six) main physical divisions.
4. The (Indus/Ganga) river and its five tributaries flow from India to Pakistan.
5. Fa-Hien and Hiuen Tsang came to India (as traders/in search of Buddhists texts).

D. Give reasons for the following:

1. India is a multilingual society
2. India is a divided into states and union territories

E. Answer the following questions.

1. Where is India located?
2. Name the states of India through which the Tropic of Cancer passes.
3. Name the water bodies that surround India on three sides.
4. What is SAARC?
5. What is the historical connection of India with Pakistan?
6. What are the geographical features that we share with Nepal?

F. Think and Discuss

What will be the problems faced by a country if it does not maintain a good relation with its neighbours? Explain with an example.

G. Picture Study

Look at the picture and answer the questions that follow.

1. Name the two rivers that form this delta.

____

2. Name the countries over which this is spread.

____

3. What is the forest in this delta called?

____

The Sundarbans Delta

Life Skills — Caring for the Environment

We have been blessed by nature with diverse physical features. It is our duty to take care of these diverse ecosystems. When we do that, we are protecting not just the nature and the wildlife but ourselves as well.

Creative Work

Have a discussion in class on the cultural practices in the neighbouring countries. What are some of the similar practices that they share with India?

Project Work

Find out the objectives of SAARC. Who were the leaders who came up with the idea of SAARC?

11 Climate of India

Warm Up

Tick (✓) the correct option.

- You are all dressed to go out and it suddenly starts raining. This means that the ______ has changed.

  a. weather ☐ b. climate ☐ c. season ☐

- When we say that tea plantation requires a uniformly high temperature 20°–30° C throughout the year with an annual rainfall of 150–300 cm, we are talking about the ______.

  a. weather ☐ b. climate ☐ c. season ☐

- When we discuss about fruits and vegetables that are available in a certain time of the year we are talking about the ______.

  a. weather ☐ b. climate ☐ c. season ☐

Did you observe from the warm up activity that the meaning of weather, climate and season is different? We have read about weather and climate in chapter 7. Weather is the temporary condition of a place and climate is the regular pattern of weather for a long period of time. When the weather of a place is more or less the same over a part of the year then it is known as season. In this chapter, we shall study about the seasons in India.

The Seasons in India

India has three main seasons: summer, rainy (monsoon) and winter.

Summer Season

The summer season in India begins from April and ends in June. Seasons vary in different parts of the country. The plains, the deserts and the plateau regions are extremely hot but the coastal and hilly areas are less hot. In the deserts and northern parts of the country hot wind blows in the afternoon known as loo.

These winds are strong and are dry enough to make people sick or ill. The temperature in the northern part of the country increases in summers as the sunrays fall directly on the Tropic of Cancer. The temperature in the hills remain cool and pleasant in summers. Coastal areas are less hot than the plains due to the presence of water bodies near them.

Rainy (Monsoon) Season

The monsoon begins from the end of June and lasts till September and it is called the south-west monsoon. The monsoon winds blow over the sea, which has been warmed by the heat of the Sun and picks up a lot of water vapours. Then, these water vapours cool down and convert into water. When the clouds become heavy, the water in the clouds fall on the Indian subcontinent in the form of rain. The monsoon first arrives in Kerala and then, gradually moves over to the other parts of the country. This is why not all the parts of the country receive the same amount of rainfall. The places which get early monsoon receive heavy rainfall when compared to places where the monsoon arrives later. The monsoon plays a very important factor in the agricultural economy of India. Most of the farmers are dependent on these south-west monsoons for a good harvest of agriculture produce.

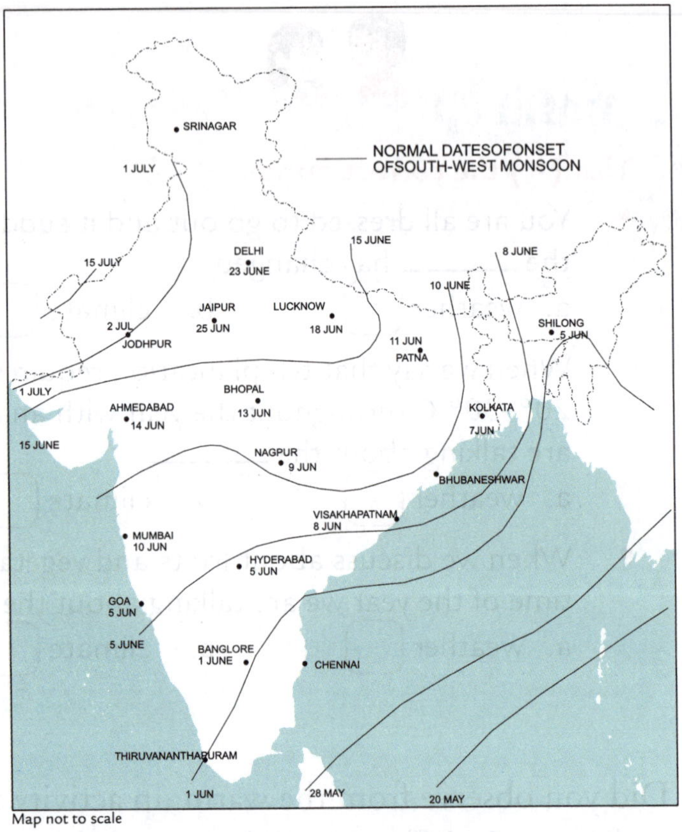

Map not to scale

Arrival of monsoon in India

Did You Know?

Most of the farmers in India are dependent on the south-west monsoons for cultivation.

Winter Season

The winter season in India begins in November and ends by the end of February. The mountains are extremely cold during the winters and snowfall at higher altitudes is common in this season as temperatures come down. Plains which are far from water bodies are cold.

A view of Gulmarg, a popular tourist destination in Jammu and Kashmir in winter

Deserts are cold at night. Coastal areas are less cold when compared to the plains in the north. In winter season, the coastal areas receive rainfall due to the north east monsoons.

In some parts of the Indian subcontinent, we can experience two more seasons: autumn and spring. Autumn and spring are short seasons. Spring has pleasant weather and new leaves can be seen on trees. It begins in the end of February and lasts till March. Holi is celebrated to mark the end of spring.

Cherry blossoms in their full glory in spring, Nagaland

Autumn begins around the end of July and beginning of August and lasts till mid-October. In this season trees shed their leaves when they turn brown.

Durga Puja and Dussehra are celebrated during this season.

Climatic Regions in India

The climate in India is different in different regions. This is because India has a varied geographical or physical features. The Tropic of Cancer passes through India so the areas in this belt experience tropical climate. India is a large country with varying topography and the climate is impacted by the physical features and the distance from the sea as well.

Chinar trees shedding their leaves in autumn, Kashmir

The climate in India can be classified into the following groups as given below.

Mountain Climate

We find this climate along the Himalayan region. Jammu and Kashmir, Ladakh, Uttarakhand, Himachal Pradesh, Sikkim and Arunachal Pradesh which lies in the mountainous region experience this climate.

Here, the summers are cool and pleasant whereas the winters are very cold on account of snowfall. They receive rainfall in the monsoon season.

Let's Talk

Ladakh is a cold desert. How do you think people live there?

Humid Subtropical Climate

Rajasthan, Punjab, Haryana, Uttar Pradesh, Bihar, northern parts of West Bengal and many North-East states have this type of climate. These are the states that lie in the foothills of the Himalayas.

In this type of climate, summers are hot and humid. The distribution of rainfall varies from part to part with the eastern side receiving more rainfall than the western side. The winters are cold and dry and the hilly areas are colder.

Arid Climate

The summers are hot and there is very little or no rainfall during monsoon season. The winters are cold during night. The western part of the country, including a large part of Rajasthan, fall under this zone. The temperature in this zone may shoot up to 50°C in summer.

Semi-arid Climate

Karnataka, central Maharashtra, interior areas of Tamil Nadu and western Andhra Pradesh experience this climate. These regions lie to the east of the Western Ghats and south of the Tropic of Cancer. The amount of rainfall received in these regions is very less, making them prone to droughts. The summers are hot and the winters are cold. This area is not suitable for agriculture and the most common vegetation here is grass. Even in the month of December, the temperature remains high. The months of March and May are extremely hot and dry.

The southern part of Punjab, Haryana, eastern Gujarat, western and north-western parts of Madhya Pradesh and southern part of Gujarat also experience semi-arid climate. The temperature here is slightly lower as compared to the deserts but the annual rainfall received is quite low.

Tropical Wet Climate

The summers here are hot. There is heavy rainfall in some areas during monsoon. Winters are dry and less cold as compared to the northern part of the country. The south-eastern coastal area has a winter monsoon.

The regions of the Western Ghats, western coastal lowlands and southern parts of Assam fall in this climatic region. This region receives heavy rainfall from May to November. December to March are dry months.

Tropical Wet and Dry Climate

This type of climate receives scorching heat in the summer. The monsoon lasts from June to September. Tamil Nadu is the only Indian state that receives rain in winters. The entire Peninsula Plateau except the semi-arid strip of the Western Ghats experience this type of climate.

Let's DO

Which type of climate does your state experience?

____

Points to be Noted

- Seasons are the part of a year when the weather of a place remains the same.
- There are three main seasons in India: summer, monsoon and winter.
- The temperature in the north increases in summers as the sunrays fall directly on the Tropic of Cancer.
- The climate in India is different in different regions because India has varied geographical features.
- There are six distinct types of climatic regions in India.
- They are the mountain climate, humid subtropical climate, arid climate, semi-arid climate, tropical wet climate and tropical wet and dry climate.

Words to Know

Temporary: lasting for only a limited period of time
Impacted: directly affected
Varied: different

Exercises

A. Write T for true and F for false statements.

1. There are eight seasons in India. ☐
2. Loo are hot winds that blow in the afternoon. ☐
3. The climate in the hills remain cool and pleasant in winters. ☐

4. All parts of the country receive the same amount of rainfall. ☐
5. In winter season, the coastal areas receive rainfall due to the north-east monsoons. ☐
6. Autumn has a pleasant weather and new leaves can be seen on trees. ☐

B. Fill in the blanks.

1. ____________ is the weather of a place which is more or less the same over a part of the year.
2. The summer season in India begins from ____________ and ends in ____________.
3. ____________ is a very important factor in the agricultural economy of India.
4. The mountains are ____________ during winters and ____________ at higher altitudes is common.
5. ____________ and ____________ are celebrated in autumn season.

C. Choose the correct option.

1. There are (three/six) main seasons in India.
2. (Loo/Monsoon) winds are strong and dry enough to make people sick or ill.
3. (Deserts/Coastal) areas are cold during the night.
4. The north-east monsoon is experienced by (North India/south-eastern coastal regions).
5. The (climate/weather) of India has an effect on the plants, animals and people of an area.

D. Put the words given in the box under the correct category.

hot,	beach,	cold,	snow,	umbrella,	juice,
gloves,	paper boats,	jacket,	gumboots,	fan,	raincoat

Summer Season	Rainy Season	Winter Season

E. Answer the following questions.

1. What are seasons? How many seasons does India have?
2. When does summer season arrive in India?
3. Why are summers so hot in the northern part of India?
4. What causes monsoon in India?
5. Explain the climate in different regions of India during winters.
6. How many climatic regions are there? Name them.

F. Think and Discuss

1. Summers are getting hotter in India now and winters are getting warmer in the Northern Plains. What is the reason behind this?
2. Why is Tamil Nadu the only state in India that receives winter rain?

G. Picture Study

Look at the picture and answer the questions that follow.

1. Name the season which is shown in this picture.

   ____

2. When does this season begin and end? ____________________
3. How is the weather in this season? ____________________

New flowers and fresh leaves on trees

Life Skills — Following a Routine

People adapt themselves to the prevailing surroundings to survive. Similarly, we should learn to adapt to our surroundings and the changes happening around us. This will help us to make the best of the situation and we will not feel left behind.

Creative Work

Collect the pictures of fruits and vegetables which grow in different seasons. Also find out which fruits are eaten throughout the year.

Project Work

Make a project on one of the climatic regions of India. Explain it with the help of examples. Also, mention about the lifestyle of people living there and the agricultural activities in that regions.

12 Natural Vegetation

Warm Up

Tick (✓) the right option.

- Trees with needle-like leaves grows naturally in:
  a. coastal areas ☐ b. mountainous regions ☐ c. plains ☐
- Coconut trees are found in abundance in:
  a. coastal areas ☐ b. mountainous regions ☐ c. plateaus ☐
- Hardwood trees grow well in:
  a. cold climate ☐ b. tropical climate ☐ c. desert climate ☐

The plants and trees that grow naturally in a specific region are the natural vegetation of a place. These may not be planted or grown by the people living in these regions. In this chapter, we will read about the different natural vegetation which grows in different parts of India.

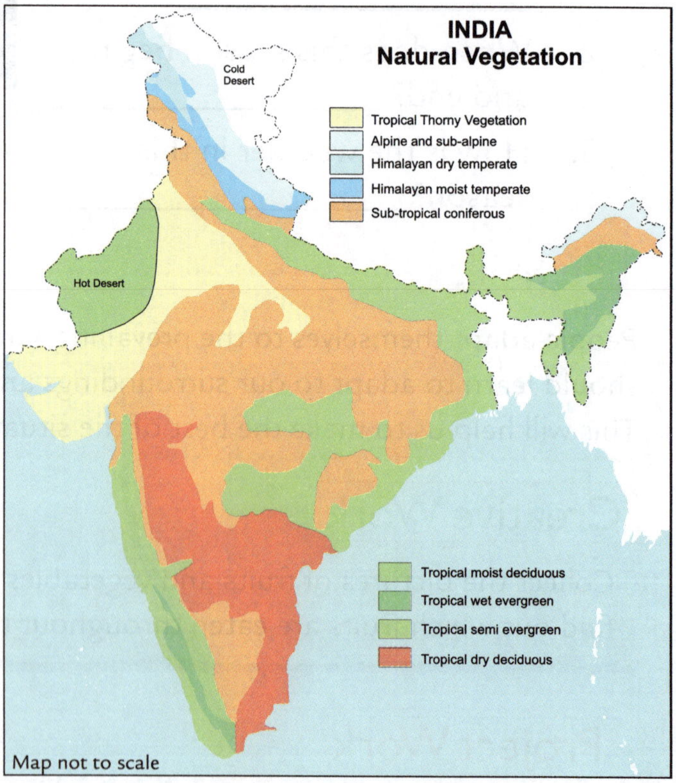

Natural vegetation of India

Forests

One-fifth of our country is covered with forests and they form the most important part of the natural vegetation in India. They are thickly covered with different trees and plants.

Forests are important to human beings as they provide us our day-to-day needs. They provide us oxygen and absorb carbon dioxide and the wood we need to make furniture for homes, schools and offices. They provide us with fruits, medicinal herbs, gum, rubber and wood pulp for making paper. Trees also prevent soil erosion and keep the weather cool. Forests are also home to a variety of animals.

Did You Know?

About 33 per cent of the plant species in the world grow naturally in India. It means that they are not found anywhere else in the world.

Types of Forests in India

Tropical Evergreen Forests

Canopy of tropical evergreen forest, Andaman Islands

Evergreen forests remain green throughout the year as all the trees do not shed their leaves at the same time. When some trees shed their leaves, others grow new leaves. These forests are very dense and covered by long trees. These trees form a canopy with the branches that block the sunlight from reaching the ground. These forests are found on the slopes of the Western Ghats, in the states of Assam, Arunachal Pradesh, Nagaland, Tripura, Meghalaya, West Bengal and the Andaman and Nicobar Islands. These forests are found in areas that receive more than 200 cm of rainfall. Some trees which can be found in these forests are rosewood, ebony and mahogany.

Tropical Deciduous Forests

Tropical deciduous forest

These forests shed their leaves once in a year. They are also known as monsoon forests. These areas receive rainfall between 100-200cm. They are found in the states of Jharkhand, Odisha and Chhattisgarh. They are also found in the foothills of the Himalayas and the wetter parts of the Peninsular Plateau. They cover a greater area of land than the evergreen forests. These forests provide us with woods that have commercial value. Some examples of these trees are bamboo, teak, sal, shisham, and sandalwood.

Montane (Mountain) Forests

Vegetation in mountains vary with altitude. The first region is known as wet temperate region and lies at an altitude of 1800 to 3000 metres above sea level. This region receives an annual rainfall of 150-300 cms. The trees found in this region are sal, teak, bamboo and cane.

Pine forests in Uttarakhand

The second region is the temperate forests which can be found at a height of 1500-3000 metres. They receive an annual rainfall of 150-250cm. Pine, deodar and spruce are found here. These are found in the southern slopes of the Himalayas and at high altitude regions of South India and North-East India.

Lichen

Moss

The third region is the Alpine forests which lie at 3500 metres above from sea level. The annual rainfall is below 100 cm. Pines, rhododendrons and birches are found in this region.

The places which are above 3500 metres are snow-covered and have mosses and lichens. Some areas are hard and rocky without any vegetation.

Let's Talk

What kind of agricultural activities do people in the alpine regions carry out?

Thorn and Scrub Forests

Thorn forest

Thorn and scrub forests cover vegetation which includes mostly bushes and trees like keekar, date and palms as these plants can survive in dry areas, where the annual rainfall is less than 70 cm. These plants can be found in Rajasthan, Punjab and Haryana. These trees have thick bark, sharp thorns and long roots to absorb water from the ground.

Tidal or Mangrove Forests

Mangrove forest

Tidal or mangrove forests are found in the deltas formed by rivers in areas that receive more than 200 cm of annual rainfall. These mangrove trees' roots grow above and below the rivers. The Sundarbans delta is formed by the rivers of Ganga and Brahmaputra in West Bengal. The trees which grow there are known as Sundari trees. The area is a UNESCO World Heritage Site for its plants and animals.

Conservation of Forests

In the past few years India's forests have been reduced to half its coverage due to continuous human activities like deforestation. This is carried out to create more space for construction activities and developing the rural areas. It has led to many problems like landslides as there are no trees to hold the soil, so the land easily gets washed away with rain and floods. In some areas cutting of trees has led to a decrease in the amount of annual rainfall received due to which various regions have now become dry. Many species of plants, birds and animals, are extinct or have become endangered due to cutting of trees, as forests are homes to various animals and insects.

Cutting of trees to free land for construction

Women planting trees in Umaria district of Madhya Pradesh

We need to control deforestation in order to conserve our forests. The government of India has passed many laws to protect the trees and to prevent the random cutting down of trees. The government has also started some programmes like National Afforestation Programme (NAP) and Van Mahotsav to sensitise the people on the need to conserve forest areas.

Let's DO

Name some things made of wood in your classroom.

____

Points to be Noted

- Natural vegetation refers to the plants and trees that grow in a particular region naturally.
- India has a large variety of natural vegetation because of its geography and climate.
- There are five natural vegetation regions in India.
- The tropical evergreen forests are found in areas that receive more than 200 cm of rainfall.
- The tropical deciduous trees are found in areas that receive rainfall between 100–200 cm.
- The montane forests are found in three layers: the first region lies at an altitude of 1800–3000 metres above sea level, the second region can be found at a height of 1500–3000 metres and the third region is the Alpine forest which lies at 3500 metres above from sea level.
- Thorn and scrub forests are found where the annual rainfall is less than 70 cm.
- Tidal or mangrove forests are found in the deltas formed by rivers in areas that receive more than 200 cm of annual rainfall.
- We need to conserve our forests by controlling deforestation.

Words to Know

Pulp: a soft, wet, shapeless mass of a material

Soil erosion: removal of upper layer of soil

Canopy: the uppermost branches of the trees in a forest, forming a more or less continuous layer of leaves

Commercial: intended to make a profit

Deltas: landform created by deposition of sand or soil

Extinct: animals or plants which no longer exist on Earth

Endangered: animals or plants which are in danger of getting extinct

Afforestation: the process of growing more plants

Exercises

A. Write T for true and F for false sentences.

1. One-fifth of our country is covered with forests. ☐

2. Forests provide us carbon dioxide and absorb oxygen. ☐

3. Thorn and shrub trees form a canopy with the branches that blocks the sunlight from reaching the ground. ☐

4. The places which are above 3500 metres from the sea level are snow-covered and have mosses and lichens. ☐

5. Tidal or mangrove forests are dense and are found in the deltas. ☐

B. Fill in the blanks.

1. ________________ forests remain evergreen throughout the year.
2. Monsoon forests is another name of ________________ forests.
3. Vegetation in mountains vary with ________________.
4. ________________ forest trees have thick bark, sharp thorns and long roots.
5. The ________________ delta is formed by the rivers of Ganga and Brahmaputra in West Bengal.
6. Forests are ________________ to various species of plants, birds and animals.

C. Choose the correct option.

1. Evergreen forest can be found in (Meghalaya/Rajasthan).
2. Deciduous forest provide wood for (public/commercial) use.
3. (Date and palms/Spruce and deodar) can be found in thorn and shurb forests.
4. The (wet temperate/temperate) region lies at an altitude of 1800 to 3000 metres above sea level.
5. The rivers Ganga and (Brahamaputra/Yamuna) form the Sunderbans delta.

D. Answer in one word.

1. They shed their leaves once in a year: ________________
2. Forests found at a height of 1500–3000 metres: ________________
3. The vegetation in this region are bushes and palm trees: ________________
4. The trees which grow in the Sunderban delta: ________________
5. A programme started by government to conserve forests: ________________

E. Answer the following questions.

1. What is natural vegetation?

2. Why do tropical evergreen forests remain green throughout the year?
3. What are the features of a deciduous forest?
4. Explain the montane forests in detail.
5. Why is India's forest area getting reduced?
6. What are the consequences of deforestation?

F. Think and Discuss

In this chapter, we learnt that deforestation has led to problems like landslides and soil erosion. What are some other human activities which has led to the decline of the natural environment?

G. Picture Study

Look at the picture and answer the questions that follow.

1. Where is this plant found?

____

2. What are the characteristic features of plants growing in this forest?

____

3. Name some other plants that grow in this forest.

____

Prickly pear

Life Skills — Empathy

In our greed to make homes and things for ourselves we are destroying the homes of other living beings. Natural vegetation supports the local animal life and maintains a balance in the environment. We should remember that plants and animals have as much right to this planet as we have.

Creative Work

Make a poster with slogans on conservation of forests and spread awareness in your school by organising a campaign.

Project Work

Make a list of some other programmes which have led to the conservation of forest areas. Also do a research work on the movements started by people in different regions of India to conserve forests.

Theme 5: The Environment–Major Concerns

13 Components of the Earth

Warm Up

List some of the things which we get from Earth.

1. ____________ 2. ____________ 3. ____________

4. ____________ 5. ____________ 6. ____________

All the things that you have listed form our environment.

What Is Environment?

The people, places, animals and plants of an area makes our surrounding. And everything that surrounds us is our environment. An environment includes both living and non-living things around us and all these things are interdependent on each other. We depend on our environment for our survival.

Components of the Environment

There are two major components of the environment. They are:

1. Abiotic components
2. Biotic components

Abiotic and Biotic components of Earth

Abiotic Components

Abiotic components refer to all the non-living things which are essential for the survival of all living organisms in our natural environment. It encompasses all chemical and physical factors present in the atmosphere, hydrosphere and lithosphere. Sunlight, air, precipitation, minerals and soil are some examples of abiotic factors. These factors have a significant impact on the survival and reproduction of species in an ecosystem.

Atmosphere

The atmosphere is a blanket of air and gases that surrounds the Earth. It stretches up to 1600 kilometres and is divided according to temperature, composition and many other factors into five layers. Closest to the Earth's surface is the troposphere followed by stratosphere, mesosphere, thermosphere and the exosphere.

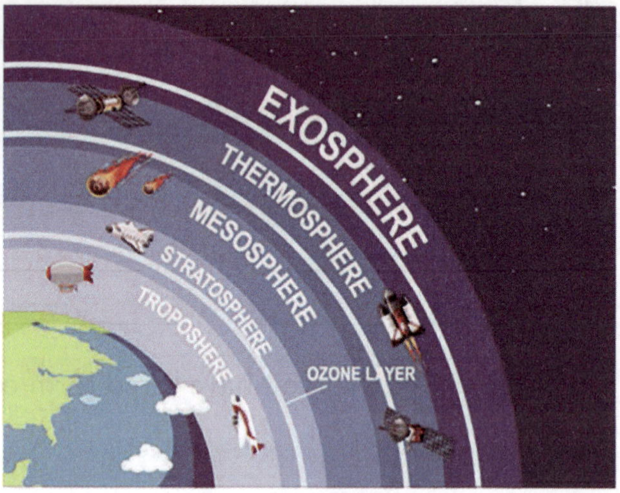

Atmospheric layers

The atmosphere is mainly composed of two gases: oxygen (21 per cent) and nitrogen (78 per cent) and other gases like carbon dioxide, hydrogen and helium. The atmosphere protects us from harmful rays of the Sun. The layer of the atmosphere that protects us from the ultra violet rays of the Sun is the ozone layer which is in the stratosphere. The atmosphere traps the heat from the Sun and keeps the Earth warm. This heating up of the Earth is called greenhouse effect. Atmosphere has oxygen and this is used by the plants and animals living on Earth to breathe.

Hydrosphere

The word, hydrosphere, is derived from the Greek word 'hydro' meaning water. This includes the surface which is covered by water on Earth. Water is present on Earth in the form of rivers, lakes, seas and oceans. Some water is present inside the Earth's surface in the form of ground water. Water is also present in the solid form like ice bergs and in gaseous form as water vapours. Water changes its form from solid to

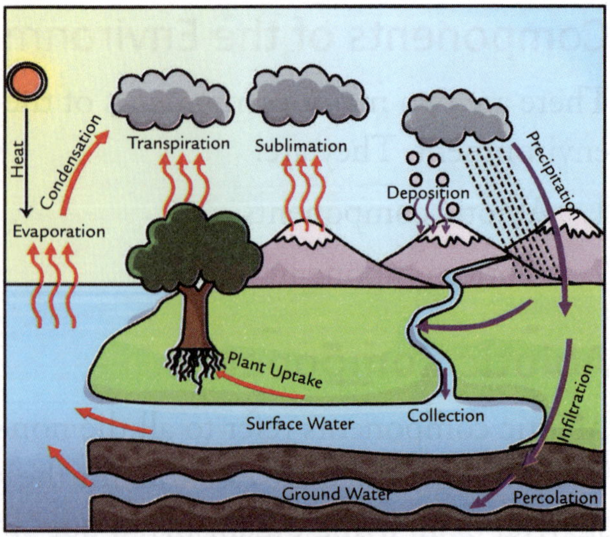

Water cycle

liquid, liquid to gaseous and gaseous to solid. Thus, it follows a cycle in which the ice melts into water and flows to oceans and seas, then this water evaporates due to the heat of the Sun and become water vapours. This water again falls onto Earth in the form of rain. This cycle of water is known as the water cycle. This water cycle plays a major role in distributing water on the surface of the Earth. The hydrosphere covers 70 per cent of the Earth's surface and is home to many plants and animals.

Lithosphere

Lithosphere is the outer layer of the Earth's surface. It includes the crust and upper mantle. The top layer of the lithosphere is soil which is important for living organisms like plants as it helps them to grow. It is also home to many creatures like worms. It is an irregular surface with various landforms such as mountains, plateaus, desert, plains and valleys. Lithosphere provides us forests, grassland for grazing, land for agriculture and human settlements. It is also a treasure of various minerals.

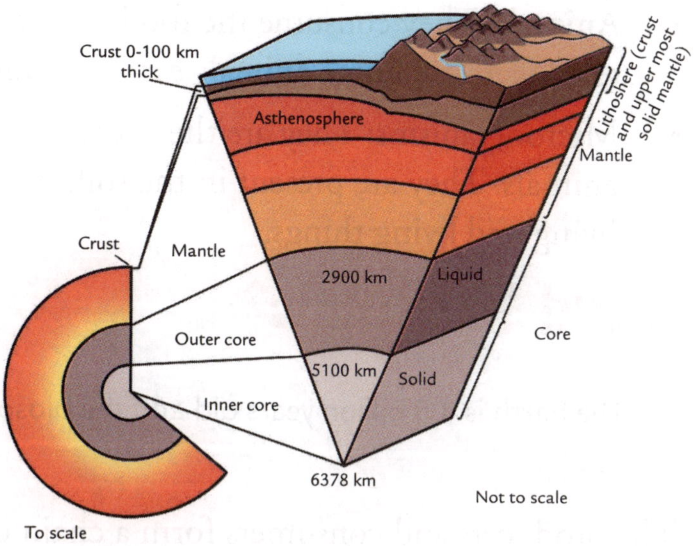

Lithosphere

Let's Talk

What are some actions that make soil lose its fertility?

Let's DO

Name some minerals that we mine from the lithosphere.

____

Biotic Components

Bio means 'life'. It includes all the living things like microorganisms, animals, humans beings and plants. All these are interdependent on each other and support each other to sustain life on Earth. The lithosphere, the hydrosphere and the atmosphere are also part of the biosphere.

Biotic components are classified as:

Producers Consumers Decomposers

- Plants: They are the primary producers as they produce food on their own and for this reason they are known as producers.
- Animals: They consume the food provided by the plants, so they are known as consumers. Some animals eat other animals.
- Microorganisms: They are the decomposers and decompose dead plants and animals. They are present in the soil, in the air or on the surfaces of non-living and living things.

Did You Know?

The Earth is 4.5 billion years old and the biosphere is about 3.5 billion years old.

The producers and consumers form a chain of interdependence in nature which is known as food web.

Points to be Noted

- The environment includes both living and non-living things around us.
- Abiotic components include all non-living things of the environment.
- The atmosphere is a blanket of air and gases that surrounds the Earth.
- Hydrosphere includes the surface which is covered by water on Earth.
- Lithosphere is the outer layer of the Earth's surface and includes the crust and upper mantle.
- Biotic components include all the living things like microorganisms, animals, humans beings and plants.

Words to Know

Interdependent: depending on each other

Ecosystem: a group of living organisms that live in and interact with each other in a specific environment

Ultra violet: a light that causes the skin to turn darker and that can be dangerous in large amounts

Evaporates: to change from liquid to gas

Crust: the hard top layer of the lithosphere

Mantle: the part of the Earth between the surface (crust) and the centre (core)

Exercises

A. Write T for true and F for false sentences.

1. The people, places, animals and plants of an area make our surrounding. ☐
2. We are not dependent on our environment for our survival. ☐
3. Biotic components include all the non-living elements of environment. ☐
4. The atmosphere protects us from harmful rays of the Sun. ☐
5. The amount of water which is present on Earth is not lost anywhere, it just changes its forms. ☐

B. Fill in the blanks.

1. Sunlight, air, precipitation, minerals and soil are some examples of ______________ factors.
2. The heating up of the Earth's atmosphere is called ______________.
3. Water is also present in the solid form like ______________ and in ______________ form as water vapours.
4. ______________ is also a treasure of various minerals.
5. The producers and consumers form a chain of interdependence in nature which is known as ______________.

C. Choose the correct option.

1. All living and non-living thing are (independent of/interdependent on) each other.
2. There are (two/three) major components of the environment.
3. Lithosphere is the (biotic/abiotic) component of Earth.
4. Water present in rivers, lakes and seas (evaporates/condenses) due to the heat of the Sun.
5. The (top/bottom) layer of the lithosphere is soil.

D. Answer the following in one or two words.

1. The blanket of air and gases that surrounds the Earth: ______________
2. The layers into which the atmosphere is divided: ______________
3. The atmospheric layer closest to the Earth: ______________
4. The layer that protects us from the ultra violet rays of the Sun: ______________
5. The layer where ozone is found: ______________

E. Answer the following questions.

1. What is environment?
2. What are the two important components of the environment? Explain in detail.
3. What is atmosphere? How is it a useful component of environment?
4. What is lithosphere? How is it important to us?
5. What are the biotic components of environment? How are they dependent on each other?

F. Think and Discuss

Why do you think the water cycle is important for all the living beings on Earth?

G. Picture Study

Look at the picture and answer the questions that follow.

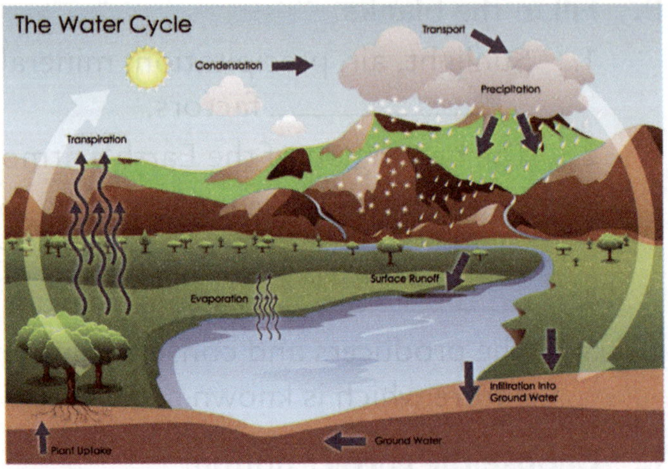

1. What is evaporation?

____

2. What is condensation?

____

3. What is precipitation?

____

Life Skills — Concern for the Environment

The ozone layer is getting depleted as a consequence of human activities. We need to save it before it's too late. How do you think we can do so?

Creative Work

World Environment Day is celebrated on June 5 every year. Prepare a PPT on the theme 'Let's Save Our Environment'.

Project Work

Make a model of all the components of the environment existing together and also show their dependence on each other.

14 Interdependence of Regions

Warm Up

Look at the pictures and answer the questions.

What India Imports

Crude oil

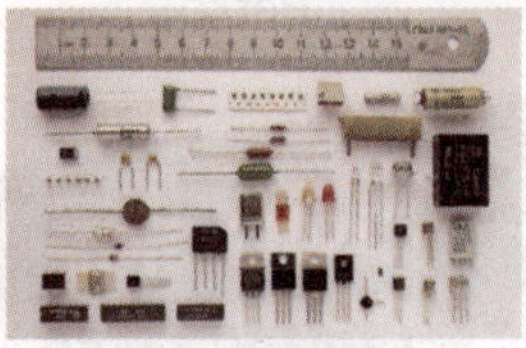

Electronic components

What India Exports

Pharmaceuticals

Fabrics

- Why does India import crude oil and electronic components? ____________
- Why can India export pharmaceuticals and fabric? ____________

Interdependence of People

From the above activity, we understand that not everything that a country needs is available in that country. So we have to import some products and there are certain things that we produce in abundance which other countries need, so we export those products. In the previous chapter, we learnt that producers and consumers form a food chain in nature. Similarly, there are different chains of independence that connect people who live in different parts of the world. People depend on each other to complete their needs. This is known as interdependence. This dependence could be on families, on towns, and even on countries. When countries are dependent on each other, it is called global interdependence.

Human beings are interdependent on each other through trade. People sell the goods they produce in exchange for money. With this money they buy things of their own requirement.

These are some instances of how interdependent we are:

- Everyone needs food to survive but not every one of us grow crops on our own. We buy it from the market. In the market, farmers sell their crops and livestock and get money in return. They then, buy the things like seeds, tractors and fertilizers that are required to grow more crops.
- Vehicles run on petrol and diesel but only some countries have good reserves of petroleum. West Asia or Middle East has the largest petroleum reserves of the world, which is about 60 per cent of the world's oil reserves. Other countries import the petroleum they need from West Asian countries and in return they take crops from other countries.

Petrol

- The US has some of the biggest IT companies in the world and to run these companies they hire people from different countries.

Google office in the US

Electronic goods

- Many countries like China and Japan export electronic goods to other countries.
- In the case of the COVID-19 vaccines also we saw interdependency. The vaccine developed by the University of Oxford and AstraZeneca was manufactured in India for Indians. It was also supplied to a large number of low- and middle-income countries around the world.

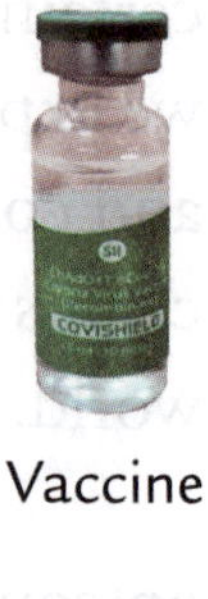

Vaccine

In trade, the resources and goods must be exchanged smoothly between producers and consumers. If any part of the chain breaks due to external conflicts it will have a wide impact on the whole chain.

Take the case of the vaccine that we discussed above. For some time, the distribution of the vaccines in India were disrupted as the supply of the raw materials were delayed from the US. Fortunately, the supply picked up soon.

Around the world, people are facing shortages of many products. Cambodia had to shut one-third of its garment factories because of shortage of fabrics from China. Myanmar, Bangladesh, Thailand, Pakistan and other countries are experiencing similar China-related shortages. Factories have started production in China again, but it will take some time to replenish the stock for these countries to start exporting again on the same scale as before the pandemic.

Let's DO

What were some of the things in short supply during the lockdown in your area? Name a few of the items.

____

Impacts of Local Events on Global Environment

Any action that takes place in a corner of the world eventually leads to a large impact as the world has become closer now with advanced means of transport.

- The case in point is COVID-19. It was first reported in December 2019 in the Wuhan city of China and soon after, the virus had spread to each and every continent by 28 February, 2020. So much so, that the entire world was under a lockdown at one point of time or the other to control the pandemic. With the advancement in transportation and with people travelling to different parts of the world, we witnessed how a local outbreak, in no time, paralysed the entire world.

A city under lockdown

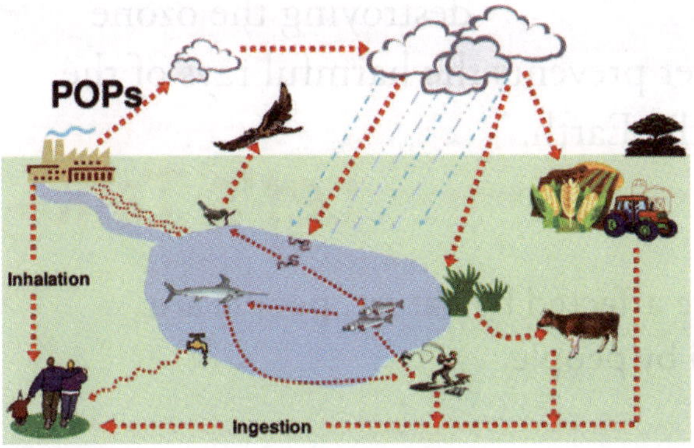

- Farmers and many industries use toxic chemicals known as persistent organic pollutants (POP). These are used as fertilizers and in industrial chemicals. Sometimes it is produced during volcanic eruptions. This gets carried to other parts of the world through wind and water and ends up having an impact on the health of the people and the environment.

- Excessive burning of fuels and cutting down of trees have adversely affected the climate globally. It has impacted the population of coral reefs in seas and oceans.

Coal

- The rapidly increasing human population has caused an imbalance in nature and has increased the interdependence of different parts of the world on each other. Fossil fuels and minerals like coal, petroleum and iron ore are getting exhausted rapidly.
- Chlorofluorocarbons (CFCs) are non-toxic, non-flammable chemicals containing atoms of carbon, chlorine and fluorine. They are used in the manufacture of aerosol sprays, blowing agents for foams and packing materials, as solvents and as refrigerants. CFCs are safe to use in most applications and are inert in the lower atmosphere. But when they reach the upper atmosphere or stratosphere, they undergo a change. Some of the released chlorine becomes active in destroying the ozone layer in the stratosphere. The ozone layer prevents the harmful rays of the Sun which causes skin cancer to reach the Earth.

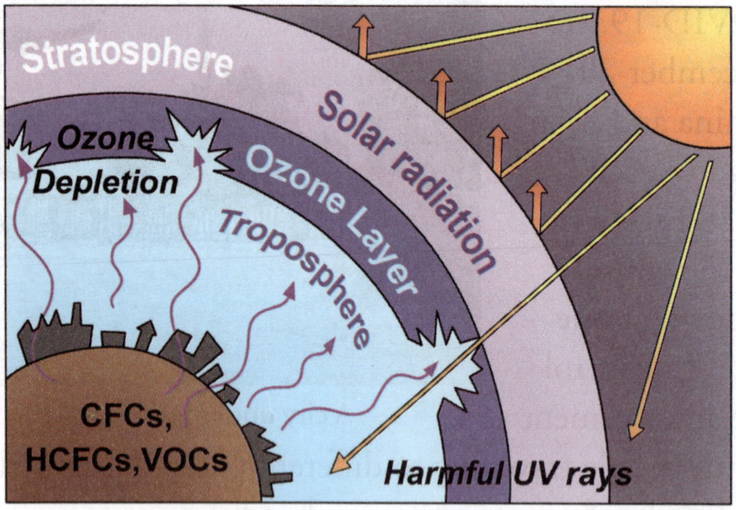

CFCs affecting Earth's surface

Let's Talk

Name some events after which people are affected by nature, people are affected by people and nature is affected by people.

Global Warming

We burn fossil fuels like coal and petroleum to produce a lot of energy which is then used to run machines. During the burning of fossil fuels some gases are released which cause pollution in the environment. Gases like carbon dioxide when present in the environment do not allow the heat of the Sun to escape from the atmosphere, thus making Earth hotter and increasing its temperature. This increase in temperature of the Earth's atmosphere is known as global warming.

These are some effects of global warming:

Meltwater gushes from an ice cap on the island of Nordaustlandet, in Norway's Svalbard archipelago

- In the Polar Regions, the ice caps are melting, thus increasing the sea water level. Areas which are at sea level or low-lying coastal areas are in a danger of submerging under sea water.
- The patterns of climate are changing as the world is seeing extreme weather conditions. In many places, summers are becoming hotter year by year and winters are harsh with heavy snowstorms. At some places rains have failed to occur even once in a year which has resulted in drought-like situations.
- Global warming also has an impact on plants, animals and tribal people who are dependent on the forest and its produce.

Since all humans depend on each other for survival, they must act sensibly as their actions may cause harm to themselves and others. We need to also save our environment to save ourselves.

Did You Know?

Maldives, an archipelago in the Indian Ocean is slowly being covered by the ocean. According to the CIA, the low elevation of the islands makes them sensitive to the sea level rising. The World Bank says that at the current projections of sea level rise, the entire country could be underwater by the year 2100.

Points to be Noted

- People living in different regions of the world are connected to each other through chains of interdependence.
- Human beings are interdependent on each other through trade.
- A small human action can have a large impact on the environment globally.
- Gases like carbon dioxide when present in the environment do not allow the heat of the Sun to escape from the atmosphere and increases the Earth's atmosphere.
- We should also save our environment to save ourselves.

Words to Know

Import: goods or services bought in one country that were produced in another
External: related with the outside of something
Marine: related with the sea
Pandemic: a disease which is prevalent over the whole country or the entire world
Exhausted: completely used up
Aerosol: suspension of fine solid particles or liquid droplets in air or another gas
Submerging: sinking below the surface of water

Exercises

A. Write T for true and F for false statements.

1. People are not dependent on each other for various things. ☐
2. We are dependent on farmers to grow food crops. ☐
3. A small human action cannot have a large impact on the environment globally. ☐
4. Human actions have affected the population of coral reefs in seas and oceans. ☐
5. Fossil fuels are burnt to produce energy. ☐

B. Fill in the blanks.

1. ________________ and ________________ are examples of fossil fuels.
2. The ________________ or ________________ has the largest petroleum reserves of the world.

3. COVID-19 was a ______________________ as it was prevalent all over the world.

4. Farmers and many industries use toxic chemicals known as ______________________.

5. CFCs have made a hole in the upper layer of the atmosphere which is known as ______________________.

C. Choose the correct option.

1. (The US/West Asia) has some of the biggest IT companies in the world.
2. Countries like China and Japan export electronic (goods/coal) to other countries.
3. (POP/CFCs) are used as fertilizers and industrial chemicals.
4. Areas which are at (sea level/high altitudes) are in danger of submerging under the sea water.
5. (Carbon dioxide/Carbon monoxide) causes global warming.

D. Enlist any six terms that were very common during COVID-19 period. (Hint: Vaccine)

1. ______________________ 2. ______________________

3. ______________________ 4. ______________________

5. ______________________ 6. ______________________

E. Answer the following questions.

1. What is global interdependence?
2. How are countries dependent on each other for goods and services? Explain with examples.
3. Explain do local events have a global impact on the environment?
4. What is global warming? How is it caused?
5. What impact does global warming have on the environment?

F. Think and Discuss

What are some of the alternatives of vehicles that run on petrol and diesel?

G. Picture Study

Look at the picture and answer the questions that follow.

This image shows how Greenland is losing its ice caps.

1. What is the reason behind this melting of ice caps and glaciers?

 ____

2. What will happen if all the ice melts?

 ____

Life Skills .... Choosing Wisely

We all know that electric vehicles are the solution to save the environment. The batteries in these cars need cobalt to prevent them from overheating. Now, around 63 per cent of the world's reserves are in the Democratic Republic of Congo. In most of the mines in Congo, children are employed to scrounge for cobalt as their labour is cheaper.

When most car manufacturers came to know of this practice, they stopped taking cobalt from Congo. Some have tried to used other alternatives. This had made an impact in making the working conditions safer for children.

Creative Work

Surf the Internet and gather the names of at least five major imports and five major exports of India. Discuss in the class.

Project Work

Do a research work and prepare a report on how children are employed in different factories across the globe. Also find out what some big companies and organisations are doing to speak up for the children.

15 Natural Disasters

Warm Up

Look at the picture and answer the questions.

- What do you see in this picture?

  ____

  ____

- Why does this happen?

  ____

  ____

- What are the problems faced by people who live in such areas?

  ____

  ____

The picture above is of a drought situation which occurred due to the area receiving less rainfall. A drought is a natural disaster. A natural disaster is a natural process which causes great damage to human life, property or land and causes economic loss. Natural disasters take place when there is an increase in the rate of human activities like cutting of trees, emission of pollutants from factories and contamination of water bodies.

Let us read about some of the natural disasters.

Floods

A flood is an overflowing of water that submerges dry lands. Floods take place when heavy rainfall takes place over an area or when huge waves from the ocean land on the shores. Floods are also caused when glaciers melt or when cyclones and tsunamis hit coastal areas or when there is a sudden collapsing of dams.

Kerala flood, 2018

Floods can bring enough water to submerge half of the building or rooftop of a house. In India, flooding is caused by heavy rains every year due to which many cities and villages get flooded with water. People have to suffer huge losses due to these floods.

Causes and Effects

When it rains heavily the level of water in rivers and oceans increases which comes to the surface or banks when they are unable to hold the extra water. This causes floods in coastal areas and countrysides. Cities get flooded due to poor drainage system or when it is not able to drain fast enough.

- Floods cause damage to both life and property. Houses and fertile soil get washed away leaving sediments of the rivers behind. The fields which are near rivers get destroyed as crops and soil get washed with the water.
- Floods can lead to loss or shortage of fresh water and vegetables. When the flooded water does not get drained easily and remains at one place for many days, it can become contaminated.
- This contaminated water causes many water borne diseases and increases the number of flies and mosquitoes which cause illness.

In India, Assam, West Bengal and Bihar are flood-prone areas and experience regular floods. Mumbai gets flooded when it rains heavily on account of its poor drainage system.

Preventive Steps

By studying the geography of an area and the flood pattern properly, the government can design appropriate drainage facilities and use strong materials for housing.

- Stilt houses should be made in such areas instead of huts and houses on grounds.
- Garbage should not be thrown in rivers and drains as it would choke them.
- Electrical equipment like poles and wires in such areas should be properly fixed to the ground and covered to prevent them from falling in water and causing deaths and accidents.

Stilt house

Drought

Drought in Rann of Kutch

Droughts occur when there is no rain at a place for a long time. The little moisture, left in the soil, is evaporated by hot dry winds due to which the soil becomes excessively dry.

In such areas people have do not get even the bare minimum water required for their daily activities and no crops can be grown.

Causes and Effects

- Failure of monsoon is the major reason for droughts in India. This happens when, at times, on account of climatic changes, the monsoon winds get shifted.
- Most farmers in India are dependent on monsoon rains for irrigation. When the monsoon fails, the land dries up and the crops get destroyed. This leads to loss of money and food.
- On a larger scale the total crop production of a country decreases when such situation occurs.

Rajasthan, Gujarat, Karnataka, Andhra Pradesh are some drought-prone areas.

Let's Talk

How are animals and plants affected by droughts?

Preventive Steps

- We have to collect the water that we receive during the monsoon in reservoirs.
- Rainwater harvesting is one of the best solutions. Rainwater harvesting is the collection and storage of rain, rather than allowing it to run off.

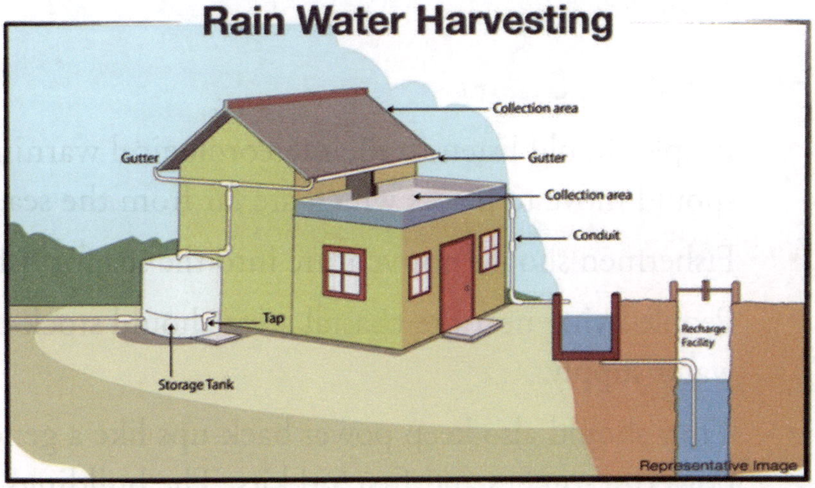

- It is collected from a roof-like surface and redirected to a tank, cistern or a deep pit or a reservoir with percolation, so that it seeps down and restores the ground water, the best method for storing rainwater.

This water can be used in case of monsoon failure to irrigate crops.

Cyclones

Cyclone

When the air above the sea becomes warm and rises upwards, a low pressure zone is created and a large, powerful and destructive storm with high winds swirls around in a circle. This is known as cyclone.

Causes and Effects

- Cyclones can also cause heavy rains which leads to flooding.
- They can move towards the banks and coastal areas and can uproot trees and houses.
- They can wash away cars and cause damage to the roads.
- Fisherman or sea mariners can drown if cyclones are not detected in time.
- Andhra Pradesh, Odisha and Tamil Nadu are cyclone-prone areas.

Did You Know?

Cyclones are known as typhoons in the north western Pacific Ocean and as hurricanes in the Atlantic Ocean. In the Indian Ocean they are called cyclones, in the Southwest Pacific basin they are just called tropical cyclones.

Preventive Steps

- People should listen to the meteorological warnings and stay indoors or should move to places which are far from the sea.
- Fishermen should not venture into the sea for fishing.
- People living near the coastal areas should stock up their food and drinking water supply.
- They should also keep power back-ups like a generator handy, along with powerful torches and first aid kits. The buildings which are built in cyclone prone areas should be made strong enough to withstand cyclones.

Landslides

Landslide

A landslide is the movement of rock, earth, or debris down a sloped section of land. In mountains, the soil starts to move or slide downwards destroying everything.

Causes and Effects

Landslides are caused by earthquakes, heavy rainfall, volcanic eruptions, improper land use and deforestation.

In the mountains the major causes of landslides are heavy rainfall and deforestation. The roots of the trees hold the soil securely. The lessening number of trees results in the soil becoming loose, so when it rains heavily the soil slides down the slopes. States in the Himalayan region are prone to landslides.

Preventive Steps

Terrace farming

- More trees should be planted.
- Terrace farming should be practised in hilly areas.
- During the rainy season people should be shifted to safer areas.

Earthquakes

Impact of an earthquake

The sudden shaking of the Earth's surface is known as earthquake. They are difficult to predict and can cause a lot of damage to property and life.

Causes and Effects

- The inside of the Earth has molten rocks and gases. When two blocks of rock slide against each other or when the molten rocks and gases heat the Earth's surface from inside, it comes out and it can be felt by the shaking of the Earth.

- The point on the surface of the Earth that is directly above the underground point (called the focus) where the seismic rupture begins is the epicentre.
- Areas around the epicentre are the ones most impacted by the earthquake.
- The places which are at some distance also feel some tremors if the earthquake is very strong.

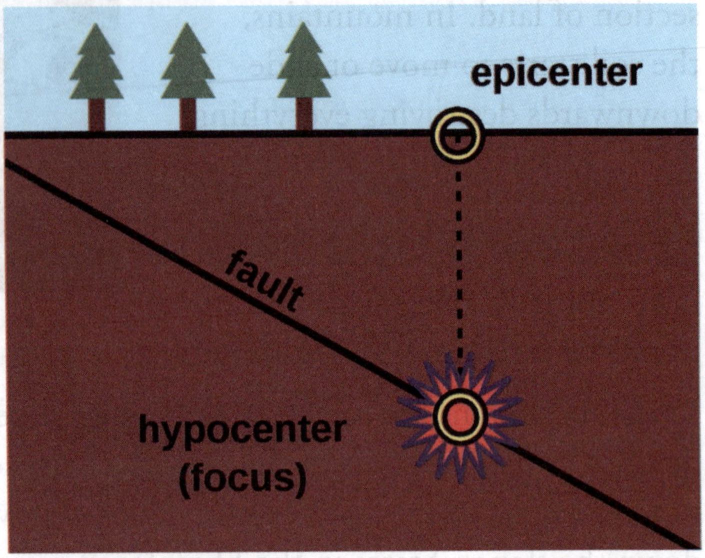

- Buildings can collapse and people can get buried under debris which causes death.
- Houses, roads and buildings can crack.
- In the mountains,earthquakes can cause landslides.

The Himalayas and the North-East India are prone to earthquakes. Some parts of Deccan and Western India and Andaman and Nicobar Islands are also earthquake prone areas.

Let's Talk

Why are earthquakes difficult to predict?

Preventive Measures

Earthquake monitoring centres should be set-up to send out timely warnings for aftershocks.

- After an earthquake of massive intensity there are aftershocks that follow. Areas prone to earthquakes should not construct high-storeyed buildings. In these areas, sturdy materials should be used for construction.
- We should run towards an open ground or take shelter under anything that has a safe roof.
- If we are inside our homes when an earthquake occurs, we should take cover under a table for protection and stay away from the windows and from furniture that can fall on us.

Let's DO

Tick (✓) the correct options.

- Where do landslides take place?
  Hilly areas ☐ Plains ☐
- Where do floods occur?
  Hilly areas ☐ Plains ☐

Volcanic Eruptions

A volcano is a mountain which has a rupture on the Earth's crust. The hot gases or molten rock known as lava is forced out through it. The thrown-out lava is said to be a volcanic eruption.

Volcanic eruption

Did You Know?

The Barren Island volcano, India's only active volcano, is in the Andaman and Nicobar Islands.

Causes and Effects

When the heat inside the Earth creates pressure due to the presence of gases and chemical reactions taking place, it escapes through the bursting of the volcano. The cracks formed during the eruption are known as vents. Volcanic eruptions occur after hundreds of years. The molten rock or lava which comes out from the vent becomes hard greyish-black rock after cooling down. The gases which are released during the eruption are poisonous and can lead to death. The hot lava runs down the mountains and can destroy everything on its way. That is why areas near volcanoes do not have vegetation and wildlife.

Preventive Measures

- People who live near eruption prone areas should be shifted to safer places and agencies should give out timely warnings for evacuations.
- People should always stay alert for these warnings.

- Low lying areas must be avoided as the lava spills into these areas.
- People must cover themselves with face masks and goggles as the ash flies all around the affected area.

Points to be Noted

- Natural disasters are natural phenomena that destroy property and life.
- Floods, drought, cyclones, earthquakes, tsunamis and volcanic eruptions are all natural disasters.
- Flood is the overflowing of water onto a dry land due to heavy rainfall.
- Drought is the situation when the soil gets extremely dry due to no rain for a long time.
- Cyclones are strong heavy winds that swirl over the oceans and cause heavy damage.
- Landslide is the mass movement of rocks or soil down the slope which occurs due to heavy rain or earthquake.
- Earthquake is the sudden shaking of Earth's surface.
- A volcano is a mountain which has a big opening at the top through which gases and hot lava comes out.

Words to Know

Disaster: a sudden calamity or accident that causes damage to life and property

Economical: giving good value or return in relation to the money and time invested

Emissions: the production and discharge of gases

Pollutants: substances that pollute something

Contamination: the action or state of making or being made impure by polluting or poisoning

Submerge: sink down under the surface of water

Collapsing: suddenly fall down

Drainage: the removal of surface water through pipes

Stilt houses: houses raised on poles over the surface of the soil or a body of water

Evaporate: turn from liquid into vapour

Terrace farming: method of growing crops on sides of hills or mountains by building terraces on the slope

Rupture: break or burst suddenly

Evacuation: removing people from a dangerous to a safe place

Exercises

A. Write T for true and F for false sentences.

1. Floods help in the increase of drinking water. ☐
2. Farmers are affected by droughts as crops get destroyed. ☐
3. During cyclones people should go fishing and surfing. ☐
4. Epicentre is the area on the surface of the Earth that is directly above the focus underground. ☐
5. The gases which are released during the volcanic eruptions are poisonous. ☐

B. Fill in the blanks.

1. Floods are a consequence of ________________ and ________________.
2. Failure of ________________ is the major reason for drought in India.
3. People are warned to ________________ or to ________________ to places which are far from the sea during cyclones.
4. In mountains the major causes of landslides are ________________ and ________________.
5. ________________ should be practised in hilly areas to decrease landslides.
6. The sudden shaking of the Earth's surface is known as ________________.

C. Choose the correct option.

1. (Cities/Villages) get flooded due to poor drainage system.
2. (Rajasthan/Meghalaya) is prone to droughts.
3. (Cyclones/Landslides) can also cause heavy rains which leads to flooding.
4. (Earthquakes/Cyclones) cause landslides.
5. People must wear face masks and goggles during (landslides/volcanic eruptions).

D. Give Reasons

1. Stilt houses are build in flood prone areas
2. Rain water harvesting is important
3. During an earthquake people should come out to open areas
4. Wearing masks and goggles are important after a volcanic eruption

E. Answer the following questions.

1. What do you mean by natural disasters?
2. Explain what causes floods.
3. What measures should be taken to avoid drought?
4. What are the reasons behind landslides?
5. What is an earthquake? Why do earthquakes occur?
6. Explain volcanic eruption in detail.

F. Think and Discuss

Of the natural disasters that we discussed, which are the ones that are the direct result of human actions? What should we do collectively to prevent it?

G. Picture Study

Look at the picture and answer the questions that follow.

1. What is shown in the picture?

   ____

2. Why is it important to conserve water?

   ____

   ____

3. Name some places where this is practised in India.

   ____

Life Skills — Being Prepared

Organise an earthquake drill in your class. Also learn the basic treatment to be given for fractures, sprains, burns and wounds.

Creative Work

Divide the class into groups and each group must prepare a presentation on any one of the natural disasters you have read in this chapter. Take examples from real life events.

Project Work

Take a physical map of India and mark the areas which are prone to different natural disasters. Show those places with different symbols and colours.

Theme 6: Natural Resources

16 Renewable and Non-Renewable Resources

Warm Up

Which of these natural resources will never end or can be restored easily? Tick (✓) the options.

Water

Sunlight

Coal

What Are Natural Resources?

Natural resources are those gifts of nature which are present in nature without any effort or action of humans. Light, air, water, plants, animals, soil, stones, minerals and fossil fuels are very essential to sustain life on planet Earth and meet people's need. A natural resource has a lot of value. Natural resources can be classified into two groups: renewable and non-renewable resources.

Renewable Resources

Renewable resources are those resources which can be used repeatedly and can be restored easily. They are present in an unlimited quantity on the Earth. Renewable resources are naturally restored but we should not use them extensively as they take some time to replenish. Renewable resources include sunlight, water and soil.

Water

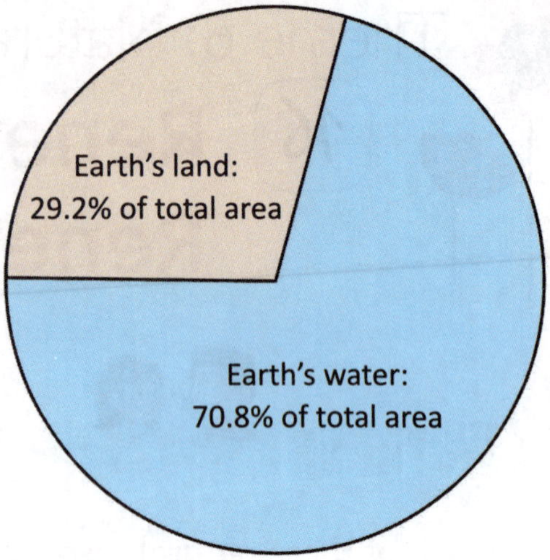

Ratio of land to water

Water is essential for all living beings. We are dependent on it for our day-to-day activities. Though three-fourths of the Earth's surface is covered with water, only three per cent of it is fit for human use. Water which is fit for human consumption is fresh water or potable water. In India we get potable water from rivers, lakes, ponds and rain. Farmers in India are dependent on monsoon rains for irrigation of crops. In case the rain fails, crops get destroyed and this has an effect on the whole nation as lack of crops results in less food production.

Let's Talk

Have you ever imagined how life will be without water?

Malampuzha Dam in Kerala

In some regions, people use water from dams to irrigate the crops. These dams are built on rivers which control the flow of rivers and store water. Some big dams in India are the Nagarjuna Sagar Dam in Andhra Pradesh, the Idukki Dam in Kerala, the Bhakra Dam on the borders of Punjab and Himachal Pradesh.

People also dig ponds and lakes to store rainwater which is then used for daily purposes. In some places, when it rains, the water seeps into the ground and reaches to the bottom of the ground where there is a layer of stones and rocks. The water that is collected in this layer is ground water and is used by people in the rural areas. They dig wells and attach hand pumps to the ground which then pulls up the ground water.

Air and Sunlight

Solar panels are used to generate solar energy

Wind turbines set up to produce wind energy

All living beings need air to breathe. The presence of carbon dioxide in the air is used by plants to make food and the nitrogen present in the air is fixed in the soil by the bacteria which is then taken up by the plants through the roots. Horizontal moving air is called wind. This wind is used to generate electricity through windmills. Wind turbines are huge fans that convert the energy of the blowing winds into electricity which is further used to pump water and for grinding grains.

Let's Talk

Which source of energy is non-polluting–wind or wood? Discuss in class.

When our skin is exposed to the direct rays of the Sun, the energy from it helps the skin to produce vitamin D. This vitamin makes our teeth and bones strong. It also gives us light to see objects clearly during the day. The heat energy from sunlight, which is called solar energy, is converted to generate electricity. This is done by installing solar panels. This energy is then used to cook food in solar cookers or to light battery lamps and torches.

Solar and wind energy are environment friendly, that means they do not cause pollution.

Soil

Soil is the top layer of the Earth's surface and is formed from weathering of rocks. It is made up of mineral particles, organic materials and living organisms. Plants and trees grow in this layer.

Soil differs from place to place depending on the geography and climatic conditions of that place. India has various kinds of soil.

The soil which is found in the Himalayas and the north-east region of India is called mountain soil. It is not very fertile.

Mountain soil

Desert soil

Desert soil is sandy and does not hold much water. It is found in Rajasthan, Gujarat and the coastal areas of Odisha and Tamil Nadu.

Alluvial soil is carried by the rivers and brought to the plains which is extremely fertile. The great Northern Plains and the Coastal Plains have alluvial soil. It is also found in West Bengal.

Alluvial Soil

Black Soil

Black soil has a lot of clay and is fine and fertile. It is found in the western and central India.

Red soil is rich in red iron chemicals and is found in the Deccan Plateau. The red soil of the valleys and plains is very fertile.

Red Soil

Laterite Soil

Laterite soil is found in the hilly regions of South India and North-East. This soil is rich in aluminum and is not very fertile.

Though India has a rich variety of soil, the top layer gets washed away by wind and rain and get eroded. This is called soil erosion. Deforestation and overgrazing of land by the animals are responsible for the washing away of the soil.

Did You Know?

It takes 500 years to produce just under an inch of topsoil, this is the most productive layer of soil.

Plants and Animals

Forests are very important for us. They provide us with valuable things which are necessary to lead a healthy and prosperous life. The natural vegetation of a place is not only helpful to us but is also home to various species of animals, birds and insects. Human activities are destroying the natural vegetation which is resulting in climate change. We need to preserve the natural vegetation before it's too late.

Biodiversity

The birds and animals present around us are also important to create a balance in the environment. India has a large variety of forests and bio diversities where different species of animals like monkeys, spiders and snakes are found.

These animals and birds are being hunted or killed by humans from hundreds of years for their skin, fur, wings and horns. This has disturbed the ecological balance of nature and the food chain.

Food chain

The given diagram shows that human beings, plants and animals are interconnected.

Let's DO

Name some plants, birds and animals which have become extinct due to human activities.

1. Plants: ________________________

2. Birds: ________________________

3. Animals: ________________________

Non-Renewable Resources

Resources that cannot be restored easily are non-renewable resources. They take millions of years to be replenished under the Earth. Fossil fuels and minerals are non-renewable resources.

Fossil Fuels

Petroleum, coal and natural gas are fossil fuels. They have been formed from the remains of plants and animals which were buried millions of years ago. These fuels contain carbon and hydrogen, which can be burnt for energy.

Coal mine complex, Dhanbad

Coal is a material usually found in sedimentary rock deposits where rocks and dead plants and animal matter are piled up in layers. The process of extraction of coal often damages the environment. Coal is an important source of energy. It is mainly used for cooking, heating and producing electricity. It is still used in many rural households for cooking and heating food. Coal is mined in West Bengal, Chhattisgarh, Jharkhand, Odisha and Madhya Pradesh.

Petroleum in its original state is found as a solid material between layers of sedimentary rocks, like shale. This material is heated in order to produce the thick oil that can be used to make gasoline. Deep wells called oil wells are dug to pump out the crude oil, which is thick and black in colour. It is refined in the oil refineries to get different products like petrol, diesel, kerosene, etc. Petrol is a major source of power and is used for running cars, buses, ships, aeroplanes and machines. Mumbai in Maharashtra, Ankleshwar in Gujarat and Digboi in Assam have oil reserves.

Jamnagar oil refinery

Natural gas is usually found in pockets above oil deposits. It can also be found in sedimentary rock layers that does not contain crude oil. Natural gas is primarily made up of methane. Almost 70 per cent of India's natural gas reserves are found in Mumbai High basin and in Gujarat and the rest is found in Andhra Pradesh and Tamil Nadu.

Mumbai High

Did You Know?

Natural gas has no colour nor odour but it is explosive. So, an odour is added to it before it is dispatched for use so that any leakage can be detected.

Minerals

Minerals are of two types: metallic and non-metallic.

Metallic minerals have metals in their chemical composition. These metals are extracted from the minerals. The metals extracted are good conductors of heat and electricity. They are malleable. Some examples of metals extracted are iron, copper, gold, silver, bauxite and manganese.

Non-metallic minerals do not contain metals. Examples of non-metallic minerals are diamond, mica, salt, potash, etc. They are bad conductors of heat and electricity and are not malleable.

Minerals	Where is it used?
Aluminum	Automobile, packaging, building/construction industry; electrical appliances and machinery
Copper	Machine parts, electronic components, electrical wires, coins and jewellery
Gold	Jewellery and arts; dentistry and medicine; in medallions and coins; as a store of value
Cobalt	Aircraft gas turbine engines, in cemented carbides for cutting tools and wear-resistant applications, chemicals
Gypsum	Prefabricated wallboard or an industrial or building plaster; in cement manufacturing and agriculture
Mica	Paints, as joint cement, as a dusting agent, in oil well drilling muds; and in plastics, roofing, rubber, welding rods
Lead	Lead-acid batteries, solders, seals or bearing; used in electrical and electronic applications; TV tubes, glass and construction

Nickel	An alloy of stainless steel, in chemical and aerospace industries
Potash	Fertilizer, in medicine and to produce decorative colour effects on brass, bronze and nickel
Silver	In coins and medals, electrical and electronic devices, industrial applications, jewellery, silverware, photography
Diamond	Mainly as a jewellery, as abrasives and for high pressure research

Ways to Conserve Our Resources

We should use our renewable as well as non-renewable resources with care. These resources are needed to be conserved as they are under great threat because of human actions. We should take certain measures to ensure that these resources do not get polluted and that we should not extract more than what is required of the non-renewable resources.

- People should not wash clothes or bathe in rivers and seas as doing this will lead to pollution of rivers and seas. Industrial waste must be treated properly before discharging it into the water bodies. Plastic items should not be thrown into rivers as it will cause blocking of the canals and will also harm aquatic life.
- Air pollution can be controlled by not burning plastic waste and fossil fuels. Emissions of different poisonous gases from different industries must be controlled as breathing impure air is harmful for both humans and animals.
- Afforestation should be done to protect soil erosion. Also, harmful chemicals should not be mixed in soil as it makes the soil poisonous and destroys the crops.
- Natural vegetation and species of different birds and animals must be preserved by putting a ban to hunting and killing of animals. Nowadays hunting of animals is a punishable offence. Also, biosphere reserves are set up by the government where animals live in their natural habitat peacefully.
- Coal and petroleum should be used judiciously as these are non-renewable resources. Instead of using vehicles which run on petrol and diesel, we should opt for electric vehicles or cycle to cover short distances.

Points to be Noted

- Natural resources are those resources which exist in nature without any human intervention.
- Renewable resources are those which are present in unlimited quantity and can replenish themselves quickly.
- Non-renewable resources are the resources which are present in limited quantity and takes millions of years to get to the form in which they can be used as resources.
- Non-renewable resources are fossil fuels and minerals.
- We need to conserve our natural resources for future use.

Words to Know

Replenish: fill up again or to restore

Weathering: breaking down of rocks and minerals on Earth's surface

Ecological balance: the balance between the organisms and the environment

Food chain: the sequence of transfers of matter and energy in the form of food from organism to organism

Refineries: a place where raw materials are converted into some valuable substance by removing impurities

Malleable: able to be hammered or pressed into shape without breaking or cracking

Biosphere reserves: protected areas meant for the conservation of plants and animals

Exercises

A. Write T for true and F for false sentences.

1. Natural resources are very important to meet people's need. [ ]
2. Renewable resources are present in limited quantity. [ ]
3. Water is used for generating electricity. [ ]
4. Solar energy is used for cooking food. [ ]
5. Hunting and killing of animals do not disturb the ecological balance. [ ]
6. Coal and petroleum are non-renewable resources. [ ]

B. Fill in the blanks.

1. Rainwater that seeps into the ground and gets collected in a layer of stones and rocks is called ______________________.
2. The presence of ______________________ in air is used by plants to make their food.
3. The heat energy from sunlight which is called ______________________ is converted to generate ______________________.
4. The washing away of the top layer of the Earth's surface is called ______________________.
5. ______________________ is a thick black liquid which is found deep inside the Earth.
6. Vehicles which run on petrol and diesel can be replaced by ______________________.

C. Choose the correct option.

1. Most of the farmers in India are dependent on (monsoon/electricity) for irrigation.
2. The energy from sunlight helps the skin to produce (Vitamin A/Vitamin D).
3. (Alluvial/Desert) soil does not hold much water.
4. (Non-renewable/Renewable) resources take millions of years to be replenished.
5. (Iron/Limestone) is a metallic mineral.
6. (Zoos/Biosphere reserves) are protected areas meant for the conservation of plants and animals

D. Match the following.

Column A	Column B
1. Heat energy	a. Digboi in Assam
2. Red soil	b. to prevent soil erosion
3. Wind	c. to produce electricity
4. Afforestation	d. horizontal moving air
5. Petroleum	e. rich in iron chemicals

E. Answer the following questions.

1. What are natural resources? How many types of natural resources are there?
2. What is the difference between renewable and non-renewable resources? Give examples.
3. How is water used for different purposes?
4. What is soil erosion? How is soil helpful to us and how can we prevent soil erosion?

5. What is petroleum and how is it obtained?

6. How can we conserve our natural resources?

F. Think and Discuss

In ancient times, people used to worship nature. Why do you think they did so? Was it because they had a better understanding of how nature sustained life on Earth and that it had to be preserved?

G. Picture Study

Look at the picture and answer the questions that follow.

1. What does this picture represent? ____________________
2. What is the use of this mineral? ______________________________
____
3. Name the places in India where it is found. ______________________
____

Life Skills — Conservation of Natural Resources

India is a country with the second largest population in the world. We need to conserve our natural resources to manage the need of every person and to save it for our future generations. As Mahatma Gandhi said, "The world has enough for everyone's need, but not enough for everyone's greed."

Creative Work

Prepare a skit representing lives of people without coal and petroleum resources.

Project Work

On an outline map of India, mark the places where coal mines and petroleum oil fields are located. Use different symbols and colours to mark those places.

Theme 7: Major Occupations in India

17 Agriculture in India

Warm Up

Name the things that are given below.

____

____

____

____

____

____

These are some of India's leading products. India relies a lot on agriculture and cattle rearing.

Agriculture

Farming is the main occupation in India. It is the second largest country in terms of farm production in the world and also the second largest producer of wheat and rice. A variety of crops are grown in India.

Types of Crops

Based on the purpose of cultivation, crops are of two types:

Food crops are those crops that people have as a staple diet. They are mainly grown for consumption.

Cash crops are those crops that provide raw material for other industries and are mainly grown to be sold to earn money.

Crops are also classified on the basis of the seasons in which they are grown.

- Crops that are grown in winter from November to April are called Rabi crops. Wheat, barley, peas and mustard are examples of Rabi crops.

Wheat

Barley

Mustard

Peas

- Crops that are grown in the beginning of the monsoon are called Kharif crops. Rice, maize, cotton and millet are examples of Kharif crops.

Rice

Maize

Cotton

Millet

Food Crops

Rice and wheat are widely consumed in India. In some places millets are also a part of the diet.

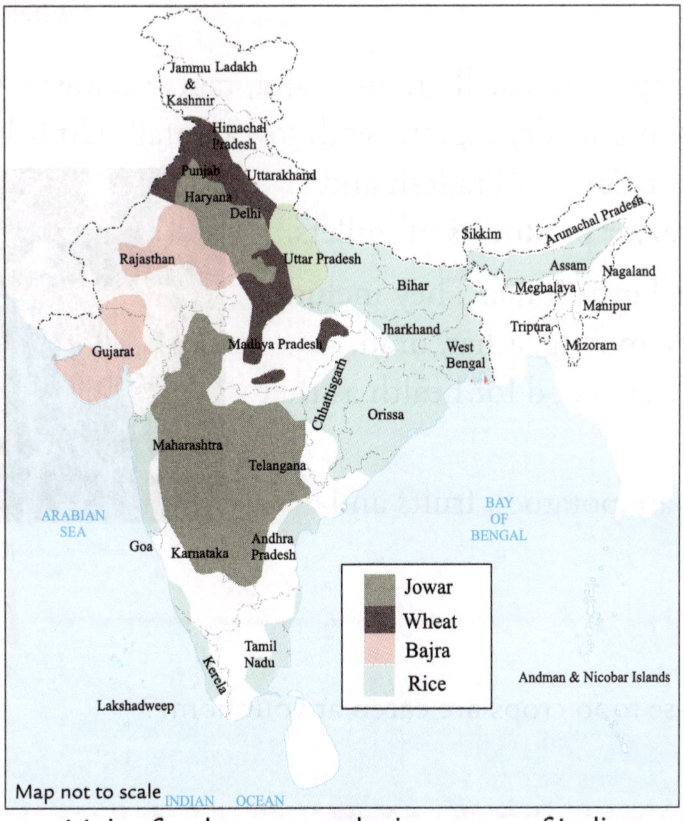

Major food crops producing states of India

Rice

Rice is grown in places which have a warm and humid climate and receives heavy rainfall. The major rice producing states in India are West Bengal, Assam, Bihar, Odisha, Uttar Pradesh, Telangana, Andhra Pradesh and Punjab.

Rice field

Let's Talk

Do you think India would be able to feed the entire country if the population keeps increasing at a fast pace?

Wheat

Wheat is grown in the winter season and it is a Rabi crop. It is grown in places with dry and cool climate like Punjab, Haryana, Uttar Pradesh, Maharashtra and Madhya Pradesh. It is the staple crop of northern India.

A field of wheat

Millets

Millets are food crops with small grains. Bajra, ragi and jowar are millets. They are grown in highly dry regions with low rainfall. Uttar Pradesh, Punjab, Haryana, Rajasthan, Andhra Pradesh and Maharashtra are major producers of millets.

Pulses are grown all over India. They include grams, beans, peas, moong, arhar, urad, masoor, etc. Pulses are good for health as they are full of proteins.

Other food crops are potatoes, fruits and vegetables.

Millets

Let's Talk

Which of these food crops are eaten at your home?

Cash Crops

Sugar cane, jute, cotton and tea are some of the cash crops grown in India. Oilseeds like sunflower and mustard are grown here. Coffee, cotton, jute and rubber are also grown in India.

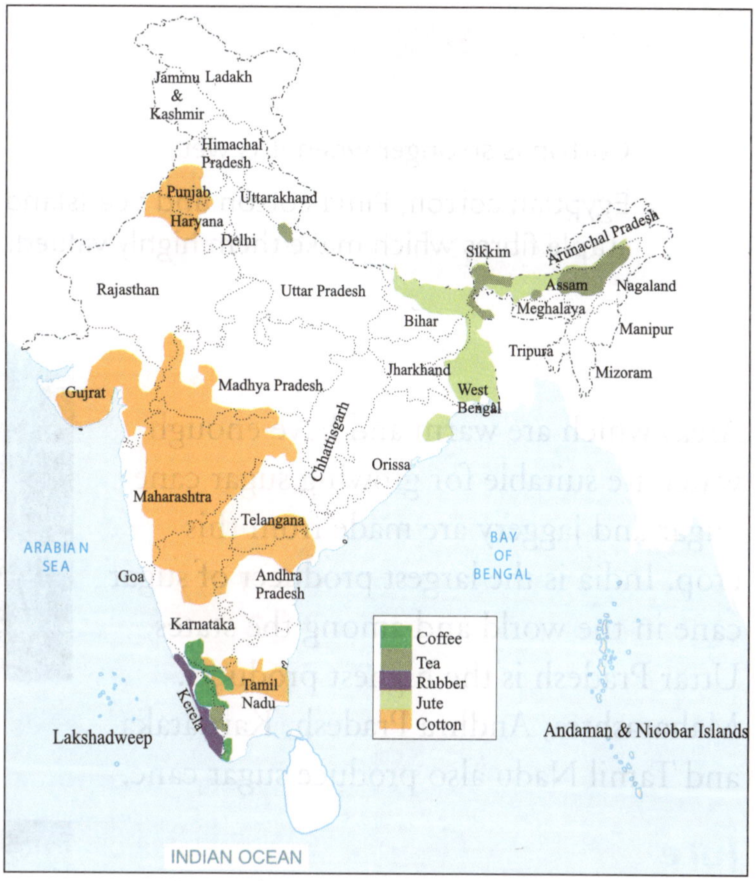

Major cash crops producing states of India

Oilseeds

Oil which is extracted from oilseeds is used for cooking food and making soap and other products. The oil is extracted by pressing the seeds in machines. Once the oil is extracted the leftover matter is given to cattle. Some oilseeds cultivated in India are sunflower, soybean and peanut. These seeds are also eaten as it is. They are mostly grown in Madhya Pradesh, Punjab, Gujarat, Andhra Pradesh, Tamil Nadu, Kerala and Karnataka.

Sunflower seed

Soybeans

Peanuts

Cotton

Cotton grows well in black soil. It needs a warm and dry climate. The cotton bolls once ripen burst and we get cotton from it. The states which are the chief producers of cotton are Punjab, Haryana, Gujarat, Maharashtra, Karnataka, Andhra Pradesh and Tamil Nadu.

Cotton boll

Did You Know?

- Cotton is stronger when it is wet.
- Egyptian cotton, Pima cotton and Sea Island cotton have extra long staple fibres which make them highly valued.

Sugar cane

Areas which are warm and have enough water are suitable for growing sugar cane. Sugar and jaggery are made from this crop. India is the largest producer of sugar cane in the world and among the states, Uttar Pradesh is the highest producer. Maharashtra, Andhra Pradesh, Karnataka and Tamil Nadu also produce sugar cane.

Sugar cane field

Jute

Jute is grown in places which have hot and damp climate. The fibre which is obtained from the jute plant is used for making fabric, bags, carpets, ropes, etc. Jute is grown in Assam, Bihar, Odisha, West Bengal, Meghalaya, Tripura and Andhra Pradesh.

Jute field

Did You Know?

Kerala is also known as the Land of Spices. The ancient port of Muziris was the hub of spice trade in Kerala in the past. Pepper, vanilla, cardamom, clove, cinnamon, nutmeg, ginger and turmeric are grown in Kerala.

Tea

Tea needs warm and humid climate. It is an important beverage crop of India. Tea is grown in Assam and West Bengal. It is also grown in the hilly regions of South India.

A woman plucking tea leaves in Assam

Coconut

Coconuts

Coconut is used for many purposes. It is grown in the southern parts of India and in the coastal regions. It needs high temperature and plenty of rainfall all around the year for its growth. Every part of this plant is used for making different products. The pulp is crushed to make oil for hair and for cooking. The fibre is used to make ropes and brooms and coconut water is a healthy, refreshing drink.

Other Crops Grown

India is the second largest producer of fruits in the world. Vegetables are also grown extensively. Fruits and vegetables are grown in nearly every part of the country. Apples are grown in Jammu and Kashmir and Himachal Pradesh. Mangoes are grown in Uttar Pradesh, Andhra Pradesh, Karnataka and Bihar. Alphonso mango, the most superior quality of mango is also exported from India. Nagpur is known as the City of Oranges. Other fruits grown in India are banana, papaya, jack fruit, pineapple, pears, pomegranate, watermelon, etc.

Development of Farming

In ancient times, though farming was one of the main occupations, it was laborious and carried out over small areas, as fields were ploughed manually or by using animals. So large areas could not be ploughed. The farmers were mainly dependent on the monsoon for irrigation. Manure and compost were used to make the soil fertile. The seeds used also did not give much yield.

As the population of India increased, more food was needed to feed the people. In the mid 20th century, changes were initiated in farming methods. Farmers were provided with loans to help them in getting machines and equipment to improve the farming methods. This led to better yield and food surplus. This was the Green Revolution.

Sprinkler

- Tractors are used to plough the fields, so cultivation is carried out over much bigger areas without much labour.
- Use of modern methods of irrigation like sprinkler and drip system saves water and labour.
- Higher yielding seeds are used, which give more produce.
- Technologically advanced fertilizers and pesticides protect the crops from insects.
- There is more yield per hectare now.

Drip irrigation

- The TV and the internet also help the farmers in getting accurate weather report, information about introduction of new seeds and prices of crops.

Did You Know?

In drip irrigation, only the area where the plant is growing is watered, whereas in sprinkler irrigation, the entire area gets watered.

Though insecticides and chemical fertilizers have helped in the growth of the crops, intake of such chemicals in large quantity is harmful for health. For this reason, many farmers are again using the traditional methods of farming which are known as organic methods as these methods do not make use of chemicals.

These are the methods involved in farming:

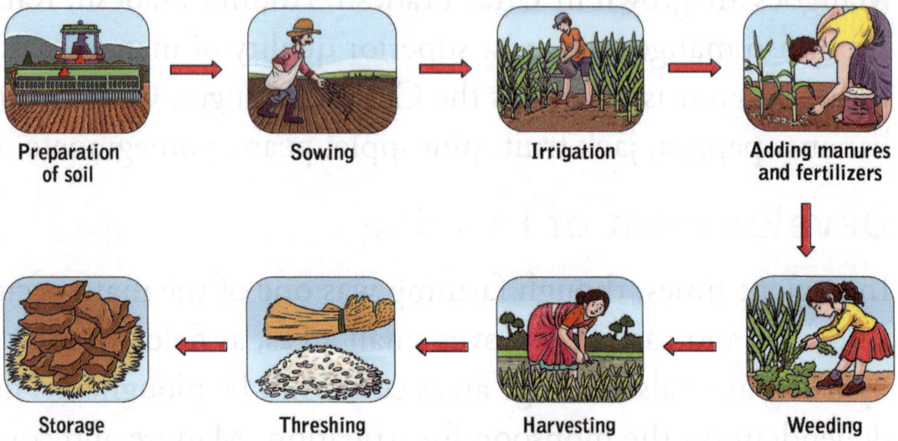

- The first step is ploughing the fields to loosen the soil.
- Then the seeds are sown.
- The seeds are watered regularly.
- When the plants start growing, fertilizers are added to it.
- As the plants start bearing the crops, pesticides are used to kill insects, rodents and fungi.. Unwanted plants (weeds) are removed from the soil.
- On ripening, the crops are harvested.

Livestock Rearing

Some farmers rear cows, buffaloes, sheep, goats and chicken in their farms for use and for profit. Animals which are reared as asset are called livestock.

Cows and buffaloes provide us milk, which is consumed directly or processed into cheese, curd, butter, etc. Cattle waste is used as fuel and for producing biogas.

Let's DO

What are some of the things that are produced from milk?

____

India is the largest milk producer in the world. This is because in 1970, the Indian government introduced Operation Flood, a scheme to link milk producers throughout India to consumers in over 700 towns and cities. This resulted in reducing seasonal and regional price variations and at the same time ensured that producers got a fair share of the profit. The success of this scheme transformed India from a milk-deficient nation into the world's largest milk producer. This is known as the White Revolution.

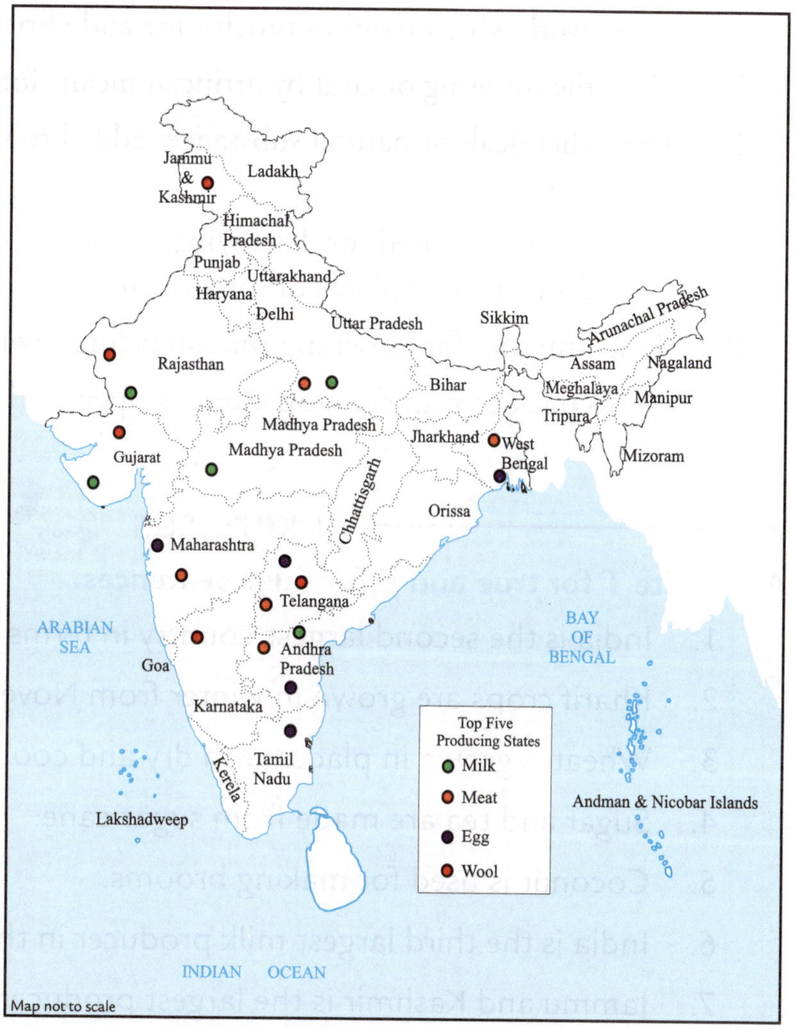

Major livestock rearing states of India

Chickens provide us with eggs and meat.

Sheep and goat provide us with wool. Rajasthan is the largest producer of wool in India.

India has a rich source of agriculture but we need to use it wisely. Farming has provided occupation to millions of people and provides food supplies to different countries.

Points to be Noted

- Farming is the main occupation in India.
- On the basis of use, crops are of two types: food and cash crops
- On the basis of their sowing and harvesting season, crops are classified as Kharif and Rabi crops.
- Rice, wheat and millets are food crops. Oilseeds, tea, jute, sugar cane, cotton and coconut are cash crops.
- The Green Revolution made India a food surplus nation.
- Livestock rearing and poultry farming is also practised in India.
- India is the largest producer of milk in the world.

Words to Know

Cotton bolls: the round, fluffy clumps in which cotton grows on a cotton plant

Laborious: work which requires much time and effort

Irrigation: the watering of land by artificial means for plants to grow

Fertilizers: chemicals or natural substances added to soil or land to increase its fertility

Pesticides: substances used for destroying insects or other organisms harmful for cultivated plants or for animals

Plough: a farm tool for loosening the soil before sowing or planting

Harvest: to puck or reap the crop after it's ripen

Exercises

A. Write T for true and F for false sentences.

1. India is the second largest country in terms of farm production. ☐
2. Kharif crops are grown in winter from November to April. ☐
3. Wheat is grown in places with dry and cool climate. ☐
4. Sugar and tea are made from sugar cane. ☐
5. Coconut is used for making brooms. ☐
6. India is the third largest milk producer in the world. ☐
7. Jammu and Kashmir is the largest producer of wool in India. ☐

B. Fill in the blanks.

1. Crops which are grown by the farmer to be sold are called ____________.
2. Kharif crops are grown at the ____________ of monsoon.
3. ____________ are food crops with small grains.
4. Oilseeds are used for ____________ and making ____________.
5. Sugar cane needs ____________ and ____________ for their growth.
6. Better farming methods resulted in the ____________.
7. Cattle waste is used as ____________ and for producing ____________.

C. Choose the correct option.

1. (Farming/Mining) in the main occupation in India.
2. (Food crops/Cash crops) are those crops which are primarily grown for consumption.

3. Cotton grows well in (black soil/alluvial soil).
4. (Madhya Pradesh/Uttar Pradesh) is the highest producer of sugar cane.
5. Indian farmers are no longer dependent on the monsoon because of improved (fertilizers/irrigation methods).
6. (Green Revolution/White Revolution) is the increase in production of milk and other dairy products.

D. Complete the following flowchart to show how farmers grow crops.

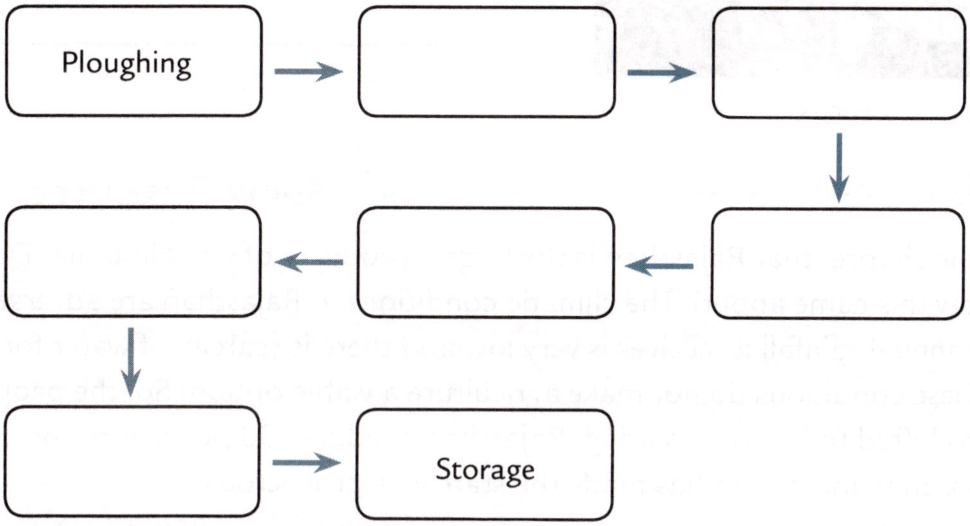

E. Answer the following questions.

1. What is the difference between food crops and cash crops?
2. What is the difference between Kharif crops and Rabi crops?
3. What are the two important food crops of India? Explain in detail.
4. Explain any three important cash crops in detail.
5. What are the changes introduced in the methods of farming which brought in the Green Revolution?
6. Why is livestock rearing done in India?

F. Think and Discuss

1. Cotton is an important fibre. What are the other fibers which we obtain from plants and animals?
2. Are natural fibres more comfortable to wear?

G. Picture Study

Look at the picture and answer the questions that follow.

Crocus

1. Why is this flower harvested?

   ____

2. Which part of this flower is valuable?

   ____

3. Where is it harvested in India?

   ____

Life Skills .... Being Resourceful

We read in the chapter that Rajasthan is the largest producer of wool in India. Do you know how this came about? The climatic conditions in Rajasthan are adverse. The average annual rainfall it receives is very low and there is scarcity of water for irrigation. These conditions do not make agriculture a viable option. So, the people of Rajasthan shifted to livestock rearing. Rajasthan produces 30 per cent of the wool production in India. This has made the state very prosperous.

Similarly, we should seek for opportunities where we are able to utilise the talents we are blessed with.

Creative Work

As the world moves towards achieving sustainability, countries are looking for ways to use things and products that are more eco-friendly. The Government of India launched the National Bamboo Mission for this very purpose. The bamboo plant is a versatile crop. It can be used as food, a substitute for wood, building and construction material, for handicrafts and paper.

Find out the ways in which bamboo is used.

Project Work

Do some research and make a PowerPoint presentation on the different cash crops which are grown in India other than those given in the chapter.

18 Industries in India

Warm Up

What materials are required for making these things?

1. Table ____________
2. T-shirt ____________
3. Fan ____________
4. Book ____________
5. Fruit juice ____________
6. Car ____________

Industries

The things which are given above are made from different raw materials in industries. Trained or skilled people work in these industries. They are important for the economic growth of the country. The more the production, the more is the economic wealth of a country. Industries provide occupation to millions of people. Most of the major industries are located in urban cities.

For setting up an industry, several things are factored in:

- Money, with which to buy land and equipment.
- Land to set up the factory.
- Location, so that it is set up near places where the raw materials are available.
- Availability of adequate electricity and water to run machines and to wash different parts of a product.
- Transportation of the manufactured goods must be available to make it easy to supply to the markets.
- Human resources, skilled workers and manpower to work on various machines.

...es of Industries

...istries can be classified on the basis of size.

- The industries that need large capital investment on land, buildings and machinery are large-scale industries. Large number of people work in such industries. Iron and steel industries that make heavy vehicles like trucks and tractors come under large-scale industries.
- Small-scale industries are those industries where smaller investment is made. Less number of people are employed in such industries. These industries use small machines or tools. Some of these are operated manually. Factories which make garments like handloom saris come under small-scale industries.

A sari being woven

- Cottage industries are those small working units that people set up in their homes. A handful of people work in such industries with basic tools and raw materials which is locally available. The main activities in these industries are weaving, carpentry, pottery, blanket making, ceramics, handmade jewellery, etc. There is a high demand for cottage industry products as the people are becoming environmentally conscious these days.

A Naga woman weaving cloth

Let's Talk

How do industries help in the growth of the nation?

Industries are also classified on the basis of the raw materials used.

- Agro-based industries are those industries which use agriculture produce as raw materials. Examples of such industries are cotton textile industry and jute industry.
- Forest-based industries are those industries which use forest products such as paper industries and timber industries.
- Industries which do not make products but provide services to customers are known as service industries.

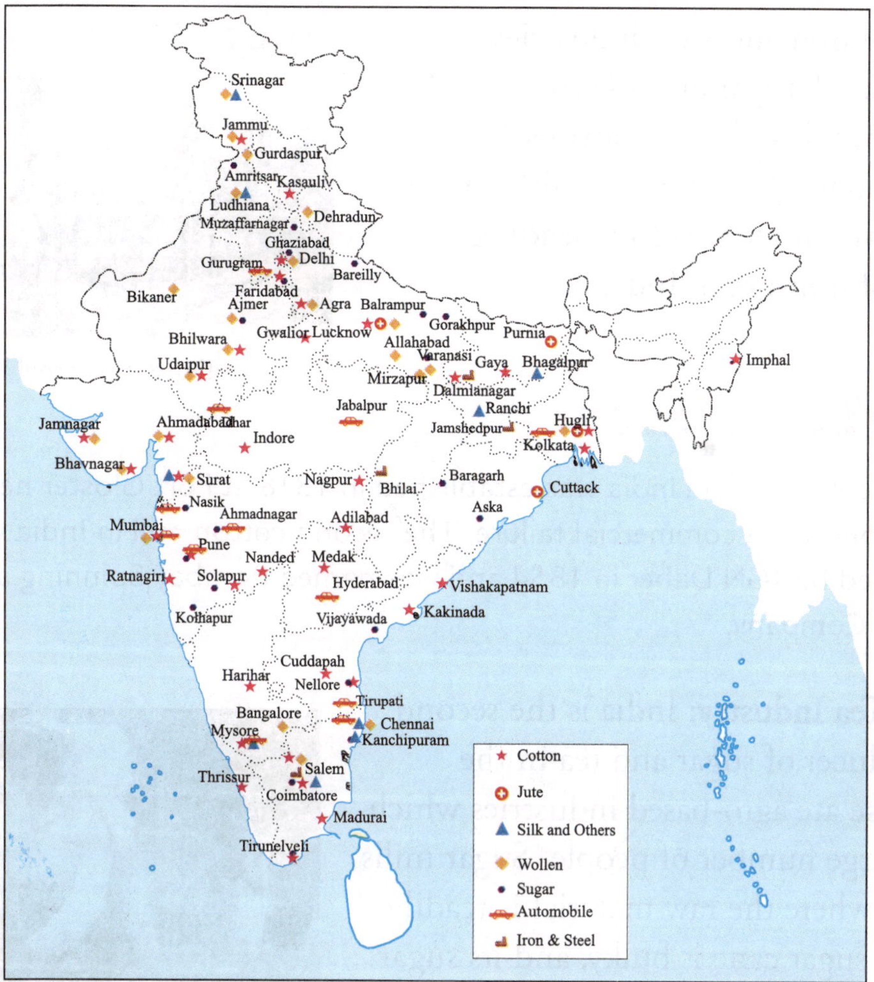

Location of major industries in India

Major Industries in India

Manually decontaminating cotton before spinning

Textile Industry: The textile industry is one of the biggest industries of India. It was set up during the British period. India is the leading producer and exporter of cotton textiles. Cotton mills and industries are found in Mumbai, Coimbatore and Ahmedabad.

Iron and Steel Industry: This industry is essential for the functioning of other industries which use iron tools and steel parts as raw materials. This industry is called the Backbone of Modern Industries as everything we use is either made of iron or steel or has been made with tools and machinery of these metals. We use things made of iron or steel to manufacture all types of vehicles, in buildings and even for household items. These industries are located near iron mines so that the raw material is easily available. Some

...re iron and steel industries ...d are Durgapur, Bokaro, ...pur and Bhilai. Chhattisgarh, Ma... Pradesh, Jharkhand, Odisha, Goa and Karnataka are some of the leading producers of iron-ore in India.

Durgapur Steel Plant

Did You Know?

The first cotton mill in India was established in 1818 at Fort Gloster near Kolkata but was a commercial failure. The second cotton mill in India was established by KGN Daber in 1854 and was named Bombay Spinning and Weaving Company.

Sugar and Tea Industry: India is the second largest producer of sugar and tea in the world. These are agro-based industries which employ a large number of people. Sugar mills are located where the raw material is readily available as sugar cane is bulky, and its sugar content reduces in haulage and time lag between reaping and sugar production. Sugar mills are located in Maharashtra, Uttar Pradesh, Tamil Nadu and Haryana.

Workers in a tea plantation

Assam is the leading producer of tea as its produces 50 per cent of the total tea produced in India. Other states where tea plantations are found are West Bengal, Tamil Nadu and Kerala.

Mining Industry: This is also one of the major industries in India that contributes to the nation's economy. India has a rich source of minerals. Both metallic and non-metallic minerals like iron ore, mica, manganese and coal are found in different parts of India.

Mining iron ore

India is the fourth largest producer of iron ore in the world.

Information Technology: The information technology (IT) industry is also known as software industry and is one of the fastest growing sectors in India. It provides various services to many parts of the world. Bengaluru is well known as a hub for India's IT sector. Hyderabad is also a big centre of IT industry.

Did You Know?

The Tata Consultancy Services (TCS) is an Indian multinational information technology (IT) services and consulting company with its headquarters in Mumbai, Maharashtra.

Service Industry: A business that does work for a customer, and occasionally provides goods, but is not involved in manufacturing is a service industry. Examples of such industries are the entertainment industry, hospitality industry, tourism, medical services, legal services, banking, teaching, etc. It also includes taxis, communication industries and railways.

Hospitality industry

Other Industries

There are other industries which are also contributing to the country's economy. These are the automobile industry, paper industry and petrochemical industry. Automobile plants are located in Gurugram, Pune, Chennai and Mumbai. Industries producing domestic appliances, electronic goods and machinery are based in Mumbai.

Paper industry is an agro-based industry. It uses wood, bamboo and bagasse, the dry pulpy residue left after the extraction of juice from sugar cane, as raw materials. Maharashtra, Andhra Pradesh, Madhya Pradesh, Karnataka and Gujarat are some states that produce paper.

Let's DO

Name some things that are made of paper.

____

Petrochemicals are the chemical products obtained from petroleum by refining such as fertilizer, rubber, medicine, cosmetics and lubricants. Some of its important centres are in Mumbai, Chennai and Haldia.

Reliance Petrochemicals is the largest producer of petrochemicals in the country and amongst the top ten in the world.

Let's Talk

What are the other important industries in India?

be Noted

ustries are the places where things are manufactured or services are ovided.

- On the basis of size, we have large-scale, small-scale and cottage industries.
- On the basis of raw materials used, we have agro-based, forest-based industries and service industries.
- Some major industries in India are the cotton textile, iron and steel, tea, sugar, mining, IT and communication and entertainment industry.
- The service industry provides services to people but is not directly involved in any production.
- Others industries which are present in India are automobile industries, paper industry and petrochemical industries.

Words to Know

Raw materials: unprocessed materials which are used for making something

Manufactured: produced on large-scale using machinery

Mills: factories fitted with machineries for a particular manufacturing process

Haulage: the act of transporting raw materials

Time lag: the time difference between two events

Automobiles: wheeled passenger vehicles

Exercises

A. Write T for true and F for false sentences.

1. Industries are important for the economic growth of the country. ☐
2. More number of people are employed in small-scale industries. ☐
3. Forest-based industries use forest products as raw materials. ☐
4. India is the leading producer of cotton textile. ☐
5. West Bengal is the leading producer of tea. ☐
6. Iron and steel industry is called the Backbone of Modern Industries. ☐

B. Fill in the blanks.

1. ____________ is needed to set up a factory.
2. India is the second largest producer of ____________ and ____________ in the world.
3. India is the fourth largest producer of ____________ in the world.

4. ____________ is well known as a hub for India's information technology sector.
5. Some industries which provide services to customers are known as ____________.
6. ____________ is the largest producer of petrochemicals in the country.

C. Choose the correct option.

1. Industries need (raw materials/human resources) to work on various machines.
2. (Farming/Industries) are the places where things are manufactured or services are provided.
3. (Agro-based industries/Forest-based industries) are those industries which use agriculture product as raw materials.
4. (Rajasthan/Assam) is the leading producer of tea.
5. (IT/Service industry) includes tourism, teaching, legal advice, medical services, etc.

D. Match the following.

Column A	Column B
1. Large-scale industry	a. mica and manganese
2. Cottage industry	b. iron and steel
3. Mining industry	c. engines and car bodies
4. IT industry	d. pottery and weaving
5. Automobile industry	e. provides services

E. Answer the following questions.

1. What is an industry? What are the things required for setting up an industry?
2. What are the different types of industries? Explain in brief.
3. What is the difference between small-scale and large-scale industries?
4. What are cottage industries?
5. Name some major industries in India. Explain any three in detail.

F. Think and Discuss

A country's progress and development is marked by the number of large-scale industries it has. It provides employment to a large number of people and manufactures goods to be exported. At the same time, these industries are one of the major polluters of the environment. So, what steps should such industries take?

G. Picture Study

Look at the picture and answer the questions that follow.

1. Which industry is this?

____

2. What is the raw material required in this industry?

____

3. Name the places where these industries are located in India.

____

____

Life Skills — Critical Thinking

With the increase in advancement of technology, things are produced on a large scale. This makes the things produced by machines cheaper as compared to handmade things. But of late, people have come to realise the value of handmade things and how they are more eco-friendly. How are handmade things more eco-friendly?

Creative Work

Do you know what product storytelling is? This is a strategy used by companies to market their products. Stories are easier to remember than facts and figures. Product storytelling is telling the story of a product such as:

- Why does the company make the product?
- Some of the unique struggles faced by the company while making the product.
- The changes that the product will make to their customer's life.

This strategy works as customers feel that such products will improve their lives in the long term and provide an inspirational outlook.

Find out some companies in India that use product storytelling.

Project Work

In 2014, the Government of India launched 'Make in India' programme to make and encourage companies to develop, manufacture and assemble products made in India and incentivise dedicated investments into manufacturing. Find out more about it and prepare a report on it.

Based on the guidelines of the New Education Policy 2020, we have attached a 360 degree holistic progress card in this book.

This progress card assesses the extent of knowledge and skills picked up by the student during the course of learning. The assessment has been customised for each chapter to get a clear picture of a student's progress. In addition to the academic knowledge, this holistic progress card also focuses on a student's socio-emotional development. Hence, this progress card reflects upon the uniqueness of each learner.

The 360 degree progress card has been designed to cover assessments of all stakeholders in a child's learning process. It includes Self Assessment, Peer Assessment, Parents' Assessment and Teachers' Assessment. Thus, this progress card has been thoughtfully created to bridge the gap between school-learning and home-learning.

360° Holistic Progress Card

Student's Name: ____________ Class: ____________

Roll no: ____________ Section: ____________

Teacher's name & signature: ____________ Parents' name & signature: ____________

Tick the correct option: = can do this = needs some help

Chapter 1: Evolution of Humans

Learning Outcomes	Self Assessment	Peer Assessment	Parents' Assessment	Teacher's Assessment
• Understands what evolution is, and how humans evolved				
• Can understand how sources help us to construct history				
• Learns how early humans communicated and survived				
• Understands about the barter system				

Chapter 2: The Stone Age and the Iron Age

Learning Outcomes	Self Assessment	Peer Assessment	Parents' Assessment	Teacher's Assessment
• Is aware of the Palaeolithic Age				
• Is aware of the Mesolithic Age				
• Is aware of the Neolithic Age				
• Is aware of the Bronze Age				
• Is aware of the Chalcolithic Age				
• Has knowledge of life in the Iron Age				

• Understands why humans used iron				
• Understands how use of iron changed the world				

Chapter 3: Evolution of Transport and Communication

Learning Outcomes	Self Assessment	Peer Assessment	Parents' Assessment	Teacher's Assessment
• Understands the significance of the invention of the wheel				
• Understands the importance of trades and voyages				
• Has a good idea of modern means of transport				
• Has a good idea of how early humans communicated				
• Has a good idea of how modern means of communication evolved				

Chapter 4: The Indian Constitution

Learning Outcomes	Self Assessment	Peer Assessment	Parents' Assessment	Teacher's Assessment
• Understands why a country needs a constitution				
• Has knowledge of how the Indian Constitution was framed				
• Has a good idea of what the Preamble enshrines				
• Understands the features of the Constitution				
• Understands what Fundamental Rights are				
• Understands what Fundamental Duties are				

Chapter 5: Features of a Democratic Form of Government

Learning Outcomes	Self Assessment	Peer Assessment	Parents' Assessment	Teacher's Assessment
• Understands the concept of democracy				
• Understands the types of democracy				
• Has knowledge about the features of a democracy				
• Has knowledge about how elections are conducted				
• Understands the importance of elections				
• Comprehends the responsibilities of citizens in a democratic polity				

Chapter 6: Locating Places on Earth

Learning Outcomes	Self Assessment	Peer Assessment	Parents' Assessment	Teacher's Assessment
• Is familiar with all important latitudes				
• Is familiar with all important longitudes				
• Can differentiate latitudes and longitudes				
• Can find out the coordinates of places and calculate time				

Chapter 7: Weather and Climate

Learning Outcomes	Self Assessment	Peer Assessment	Parents' Assessment	Teacher's Assessment
• Can differentiate weather and climate				
• Knows the factors that affect the climate of a place				
• Is aware of how human actions impact climate				
• Is aware of the effects of climate change				

Chapter 8: Solar and Lunar Eclipse

Learning Outcomes	Self Assessment	Peer Assessment	Parents' Assessment	Teacher's Assessment
• Learns how an eclipse is caused				
• Can understand how a solar eclipse is caused				
• Can understand how a lunar eclipse is caused				

Chapter 9: Major Temperature Zones of the Earth

Learning Outcomes	Self Assessment	Peer Assessment	Parents' Assessment	Teacher's Assessment
• Understands how the heat zones have been classified				
• Has a good understanding of the Torrid Zone				
• Has a good understanding of the Temperate Zone				
• Has a good understanding of the Frigid Zone				
• Has a good understanding of the effects of human activity on the various zones				

Chapter 10: Location of India and Neighbouring Countries

Learning Outcomes	Self Assessment	Peer Assessment	Parents' Assessment	Teacher's Assessment
• Has a good understanding of the location and size of India				
• Has knowledge of the political divisions of India				
• Has a good understanding of the physical divisions of India				
• Understands the geographical and historical connection with our neighbouring countries				

Chapter 11: Climate of India

Learning Outcomes	Self Assessment	Peer Assessment	Parents' Assessment	Teacher's Assessment
• Is familiar with the different seasons in India				
• Is familiar with the different climatic regions in India				

Chapter 12: Natural Vegetation

Learning Outcomes	Self Assessment	Peer Assessment	Parents' Assessment	Teacher's Assessment
• Knows the importance of forests				
• Knows the characteristics of tropical evergreen forests				
• Knows the characteristics of mountain forests				
• Knows the characteristics of thorn and scrub forests				
• Knows the characteristics of tidal forests				
• Is aware of the need to conserve forests				

Chapter 13: Components of the Earth

Learning Outcomes	Self Assessment	Peer Assessment	Parents' Assessment	Teacher's Assessment
• Understands what environment is				
• Understands the composition and function of atmosphere				
• Understands the composition and function of hydrosphere				
• Understands the composition and function of lithosphere				
• Understands the composition and role of biotic components				

Chapter 14: Interdependence of Regions

Learning Outcomes	Self Assessment	Peer Assessment	Parents' Assessment	Teacher's Assessment
• Understands what interdependence and global interdependence mean				
• Can understand how interdependence works between different countries				
• Is aware of the impacts of local events on global environment				
• Is aware of how global warming is impacting the polar regions and patterns of climate				

Chapter 15: Natural Disasters

Learning Outcomes	Self Assessment	Peer Assessment	Parents' Assessment	Teacher's Assessment
• Understands what natural disasters are				
• Knows the causes, effects and preventive steps to be taken for floods				
• Knows the causes, effects and preventive steps to be taken for droughts				
• Knows the causes, effects and preventive steps to be taken for cyclones				
• Knows the causes, effects and preventive steps to be taken for landslides				
• Knows the causes, effects and preventive steps to be taken for earthquakes				
• Knows the causes, effects and preventive steps to be taken for volcanic eruptions				

Chapter 16: Renewable and Non-Renewable Resources

Learning Outcomes	Self Assessment	Peer Assessment	Parents' Assessment	Teacher's Assessment
• Understands what natural resources are				
• Understand how we benefit from water, air, sunlight and soil				
• Is familiar with the different types of soils in different regions of the country				
• Is aware that plants and animals are also natural resources				
• Is aware of how we have benefitted from non-renewable resources like fossil fuels and minerals				
• Learns the importance of conserving resources				

Chapter 17: Agriculture in India

Learning Outcomes	Self Assessment	Peer Assessment	Parents' Assessment	Teacher's Assessment
• Is aware that agriculture is our main occupation				
• Can differentiate food and cash crops				
• Knows when and where the major food crops are grown				
• Knows where the major cash crops are grown				
• Learns how agriculture has improved over the years				
• Learns about livestock rearing in India				

Chapter 18: Industries in India

Learning Outcomes	Self Assessment	Peer Assessment	Parents' Assessment	Teacher's Assessment
• Understands what industries are				
• Can differentiate large-scale, small-scale and cottage industries				

• Can differentiate agro-based, forest-based and service industries				
• Learns about some major industries and their contribution to India's economy				
• Learns about some other industries				

Skills and Attitude

Study Skills

Learning Outcomes	Self Assessment	Peer Assessment	Parents' Assessment	Teacher's Assessment
• Listens and understand lessons in class				
• Completes assignments well				
• Takes part in group activities				

Critical Thinking Skills

Learning Outcomes	Self Assessment	Peer Assessment	Parents' Assessment	Teacher's Assessment
• Identifies different aspects of lessons				

Social Skills – Communication and Collaboration

Learning Outcomes	Self Assessment	Peer Assessment	Parents' Assessment	Teacher's Assessment
• Shows empathetic behaviour towards others				
• Displays strong interpersonal skills				

Emotional Skills

Learning Outcomes	Self Assessment	Peer Assessment	Parents' Assessment	Teacher's Assessment
• Expresses emotions				
• Understands strengths and weaknesses				

Behavioural Attitude

Learning Outcomes	Self Assessment	Peer Assessment	Parents' Assessment	Teacher's Assessment
• Expresses positive attitude towards peers, teachers and parents				
• Learns with enthusiasm				